LEGAL RESE
EXERCISES

FOLLOWING THE BLUEBOOK:
A UNIFORM SYSTEM OF CITATION

Revised Twelfth Edition

■ ■ ■

Susan T. Phillips

Professor of Law
Texas A&M University
School of Law

WEST
ACADEMIC
PUBLISHING

American Casebook Series is a trademark registered in the U.S. Patent and Trademark Office.

© West, a Thomson business, 2003, 2005, 2008
© 2011 Thomson Reuters
© 2013 LEG, Inc. d/b/a West Academic Publishing
© 2016 LEG, Inc. d/b/a West Academic
     444 Cedar Street, Suite 700
     St. Paul, MN 55101
     1-877-888-1330

West, West Academic Publishing, and West Academic are trademarks of West Publishing Corporation, used under license.

Printed in the United States of America

ISBN: 978-1-68328-100-9

TABLE OF CONTENTS

Student's Introduction

STUDENT'S INTRODUCTION

Mastering efficient research skills is more important than ever in the current legal environment. This revised twelfth edition of *Legal Research Exercises, Following The Bluebook: A Uniform System of Citation* will introduce you to legal research resources and help you develop efficient legal research skills. In completing the assignments in this book, you should become familiar with many kinds of research materials and you can use this familiarity to formulate basic research strategy. You will develop skills in using your law library and you will feel more comfortable with legal citation format.

None of the questions in this book are intended to be extremely time consuming. If you cannot find an answer, ask your professor or librarian for help. Read the relevant material in your legal research text before attempting to complete the assignments. When asked for a full citation, you are to include the case name, reporter citation, court (if necessary) and a year in your citation, as specified by *The Bluebook: A Uniform System of Citation* (20th ed.). Unless specifically directed, do not give subsequent history, weight of authority, or other such parenthetical information.

With one exception, the assignments contain four variations (A, B, C, D). Exercises A and B are written to be completed using paper resources. Exercise C is written do be completed using Westlaw, and Exercise D should be completed using Lexis Advance. The exception is Assignment Ten, which has only two variations. Its Exercise A should be completed using the Internet, and its Exercise B should be completed using Westlaw and Lexis Advance.

For this revised edition, the Westlaw exercises were written to be completed in the version available to law schools, Westlaw (formerly called WestlawNext) and the LexisNexis exercises were written to be completed using Lexis Advance.

Unless your library has a contrary shelving policy, practice professionalism by reshelving your books once you answer questions. It takes only a few seconds to reshelve the materials.

Every effort has been made to eliminate errors in this edition. I apologize for any errors that you may discover. I have learned that no matter how painstaking my efforts are in this regard, because of the republishing of legal materials, errors creep into a book of this nature as time passes. Please contact your professors when you discover a problem.

You may notice that even though I am the sole author on this edition, I have opted to use the plural pronoun "we" throughout the instructions in this book. In doing so, I pay tribute to the authors who came before me on this title, Lynn Foster, Nancy P. Johnson, Elizabeth Slusser Kelly, and J. Wesley Cochran. This work would not be what it is today without their contributions to earlier editions.

I thank the faculty and staff at Texas A&M University School of Law and the librarians and library staff at the Dee J. Kelly Law Library. I extend a huge thank you to my research assistant Kristin Brown ('13) for proofreading the original twelfth edition. I also extend my gratitude to my entire family, including mother Marty, husband Michael, and daughters Kyle and Jillian, for their support during the writing process.

Lastly, I want to thank the Judge Kathryn J. Dufour Law Library at the Columbus School of Law, at The Catholic University of America for not cancelling your paper Shepard's (before I wrote the original twelfth edition) and for allowing alums to have access! And thanks again to my family for allowing me to run over to the law library during our spring break trip to Washington, D.C.

Susan T. Phillips
Professor of Law
Director, Dee J. Kelly Law Library
Texas A&M University School of Law
sphillips64@law.tamu.edu

ASSIGNMENT ONE
FINDING AND CITING CASES
EXERCISE A

GOALS OF THIS ASSIGNMENT:
To teach you how to find cases when you have citations.
To acquaint you with the location of reporters in your law library.
To familiarize you with the rules for citing cases in *The Bluebook: A Uniform System of Citation*, 20th ed.

CITATION RULES: Read the *Introduction*, Bluepages B10.1-B10.1.4, Rules 10.1-10.5, Bluepages B6, Rule 6.1, Rule 18.2.1, and Rule 10.8.1. Refer to Bluepages table BT2 and tables T1, T6, and T10.1 of *The Bluebook*. Apply these rules as you construct the correct citation for each case.

Throughout this book, when we ask that you provide a full citation to a case, give the name of the case, the published or unpublished source in which the case can be found, and a parenthetical indicating the court and year of decision as required by *The Bluebook*. Omit other parenthetical information and subsequent history unless you are told to include this information.

The first two questions introduce you to the rules for citing U.S. Supreme Court cases. **Example: *Loving v. Virginia*, 388 U.S. 1 (1967).**

United States Reports, abbreviated U.S. in case citations, is the official reporter. Note that no parallel, unofficial reporters are listed for U.S. Supreme Court cases when a U.S. citation is available. At the beginning of table T1.1 in *The Bluebook*, read the instructions for the **Supreme Court**.

1.   If an opinion of the U.S. Supreme Court has not yet been published in *United States Reports*, which unofficial reporters should you cite instead, in order of preference?

2.   State the full citation for 529 U.S. 334.

The third question requires you to find and cite a U.S. Supreme Court case from before 1875. The reporters in which these cases were published are called **nominative** reporters, because they were generally known by the name of the person who compiled the volume. The form of citation for a case in a nominative reporter differs from the form for a case appearing in contemporary sources. Study the rules for citing cases found in nominative reporters (*The Bluebook* calls them "early American reporters." See Rule 10.3.2 and table T1.1.). Here is an example of how to cite an opinion in a U.S. Supreme Court nominative reporter: *Hughes v. Union Ins. Co.*, **21 U.S. (8 Wheat.) 294 (1823).**

Tip: For **accurate** dates of the United States Supreme Court nominative reporter decisions, **see http://www.supremecourt.gov/opinions/datesofdecisions.pdf**.

3.   State the full citation for 5 U.S. 299.

Next, you must find and cite a federal court of appeals case from a circuit. When citing a court of appeals case, always list the circuit within the parentheses, along with the date. **Example:** *Bonilla v. Volvo Car Corp.*, **150 F.3d 62 (1st Cir. 1998).**

4.   State the full citation for 641 F.3d 635.

Now, find and cite a federal district court case. When citing a case from district court, the particular court is included within the parentheses. **Example:** *Hillard v. Guidant Corp.*, **76 F. Supp. 2d 566 (M.D. Pa. 1999).**

5.   State the full citation for 571 F. Supp. 2d 548. Note: The district is listed before the state--the division, if listed, is listed after. Always include the district in the citation, never the division.

In general, for state decisions the state and the name of the court should be included within the parentheses. However, do not include the name of the court if the court of decision is the highest court of the state. Here is an example of how to cite a Pennsylvania Supreme Court case. How do you know what to include in the parentheses? Read Bluepages B10.1.3 and Rule 10.4(b) and look at the listing for Pennsylvania in table T1. **Example:** *Commonwealth v. Brayboy*, **246 A.2d 675 (Pa. 1968).**

Find 873 A.2d 501 to answer Questions 6 and 7.

6.   State the full citation for 873 A.2d 501.

Should you ever cite the official version of a case? Yes, if the case is very old and there is no regional citation. Otherwise, you should cite it **only** if you are **including it in a document submitted to a state court whose local rules require citation to the official reporter.** (See Rule 10.3.1(a), Bluepages B10.1.3, and Bluepages table BT2.) Here is our previous example cited in such a context. **Example:** *Commonwealth v. Brayboy,* **431 Pa. 365, 246 A.2d 675 (1968). Note:** We followed Rule 10.4(b) and omitted the jurisdiction Pa. from the parentheses because it is unambiguously conveyed by the reporter title.

7.   State the full citation for 873 A.2d 501, assuming you are including this citation in a table of authorities in a brief submitted to a state court whose local rules require citing to the official report volume, if available, followed by the West reporter citation.

Next, find an opinion from a state intermediate appellate court and cite it correctly. **Example:** *Maluszewski v. Allstate Ins. Co.*, **640 A.2d 129 (Conn. App. Ct. 1994).**

Find 283 S.W.3d 622 to answer Questions 8 and 9.

8. State the full citation for 283 S.W.3d 622.

Our previous example of an intermediate state appellate court citation cited in a document submitted to a state court whose local rules also require citing to the official reporter would look like this. **Example: *Maluszewski v. Allstate Ins. Co.*, 34 Conn. App. 27, 640 A.2d 129 (1994).**

9. State the full citation for 283 S.W.3d 622, assuming you are including this citation in a document to an Arkansas state court whose local rules also require citing to the official report volume.

You should be aware that not all appellate court decisions are designated to be published by the issuing court. These cases are called **"unpublished"** or **"unreported"** cases. Historically, an attorney was not permitted to cite to an unpublished case except in very limited circumstances. However in recent years, some jurisdictions have amended their court rules to allow citing unpublished cases. For example, the Federal Rules of Appellate Procedure provide that a court must allow the citation of any unpublished federal opinion issued on or after Jan. 1, 2007 (FRAP 32.1). Check your federal circuit's local court rules to determine if opinions issued before Jan. 1, 2007 may be cited. In addition, you should check your state's court rules and determine whether or not you are permitted to cite to unreported state cases in state court.

Typically, unpublished cases can be found on the court's own Internet page as well as on Westlaw and Lexis Advance.

You want to find an unpublished case from the United States Court of Appeals, Eighth Circuit. **Go to the Eighth Circuit's site at <ins>http://www.ca8.uscourts.gov</ins>.**

10. Search for the 2010 United States Court of Appeals, Eighth Circuit unpublished opinion with docket number 09-3725. Provide the proper citation to this exact copy (PDF) according to Rule 18.2.1 and Rule 10.8.1.

ASSIGNMENT ONE
FINDING AND CITING CASES
EXERCISE B

GOALS OF THIS ASSIGNMENT:
To teach you how to find cases when you have citations.
To acquaint you with the location of reporters in your law library.
To familiarize you with the rules for citing cases in *The Bluebook: A Uniform System of Citation*, **20th ed.**

CITATION RULES: Read the *Introduction*, Bluepages B10.1-B10.1.4, Rules 10.1-10.5, Bluepages B6, Rule 6.1, Rule 18.2.1, and Rule 10.8.1. Refer to Bluepages table BT2 and tables T1, T6, and T10.1 of *The Bluebook*. Apply these rules as you construct the correct citation for each case.

Throughout this book, when we ask that you provide a full citation to a case, give the name of the case, the published or unpublished source in which the case can be found, and a parenthetical indicating the court and year of decision as required by *The Bluebook*. **Omit other parenthetical information and subsequent history unless you are told to include this information.**

The first two questions introduce you to the rules for citing U.S. Supreme Court cases. **Example:** *Loving v. Virginia*, **388 U.S. 1 (1967).**

United States Reports, abbreviated U.S. in case citations, is the official reporter. Note that no parallel, unofficial reporters are listed for U.S. Supreme Court cases when a U.S. citation is available. At the beginning of table T1.1 in *The Bluebook*, read the instructions for the **Supreme Court**.

1.   If an opinion of the U.S. Supreme Court has not yet been published in *United States Reports*, which unofficial reporters should you cite instead, in order of preference?

2.   State the full citation for 513 U.S. 196.

The third question requires you to find and cite a U.S. Supreme Court case from before 1875. The reporters in which these cases were published are called **nominative** reporters, because they were generally known by the name of the person who compiled the volume. The form of citation for a case in a nominative reporter differs from the form for a case appearing in contemporary sources. Study the rules for citing cases found in nominative reporters (*The Bluebook* calls them "early American reporters." See Rule 10.3.2 and table T1.1.). Here is an example of how to cite an opinion in a U.S. Supreme Court nominative reporter: *Hughes v. Union Ins. Co.*, **21 U.S. (8 Wheat.) 294 (1823).**

Tip: For **accurate** dates of the United States Supreme Court nominative reporter decisions, **see http://www.supremecourt.gov/opinions/datesofdecisions.pdf**.

3.   State the full citation for 62 U.S. 66.

Next, you must find and cite a federal court of appeals case from a circuit. When citing a court of appeals case, always list the circuit within the parentheses, along with the date. **Example:** *Bonilla v. Volvo Car Corp.*, **150 F.3d 62 (1st Cir. 1998).**

4.   State the full citation for 675 F.3d 138.

Now, find and cite a federal district court case. When citing a case from district court, the particular court is included within the parentheses. **Example:** *Hillard v. Guidant Corp.*, **76 F. Supp. 2d 566 (M.D. Pa. 1999).**

5.   State the full citation for 622 F. Supp. 2d 908. Note: The district is listed before the state—the division, if listed, is listed after. Always include the district in the citation, never the division.

In general, for state decisions the state and the name of the court should be included within the parentheses. However, do not include the name of the court if the court of decision is the highest court of the state. Here is an example of how to cite a Pennsylvania Supreme Court case. How do you know what to include in the parentheses? Read Bluepages B10.1.3 and Rule 10.4(b) and look at the listing for Pennsylvania in table T1. **Example: *Commonwealth v. Brayboy*, 246 A.2d 675 (Pa. 1968).**

Find 697 S.E.2d 161 to answer Questions 6 and 7.

6.   State the full citation for 697 S.E.2d 161.

Should you ever cite the official version of a case? Yes, if the case is very old and there is no regional citation. Otherwise, you should cite it **only** if you are **including it in a document submitted to a state court whose local rules require citation to the official reporter.** (See Rule 10.3.1(a), Bluepages B10.1.3, and Bluepages table BT2.) Here is our previous example cited in such a context. **Example: *Commonwealth v. Brayboy*, 431 Pa. 365, 246 A.2d 675 (1968). Note**: We followed Rule 10.4(b) and omitted the jurisdiction Pa. from the parentheses because it is unambiguously conveyed by the reporter title.

7.   State the full citation for 697 S.E.2d 161, assuming you are including this citation in a document submitted to a state court whose local rules also require citing to the official report volume, if available, followed by the West reporter citation.

Next, find an opinion from a state intermediate appellate court and cite it correctly. **Example: *Maluszewski v. Allstate Ins. Co.*, 640 A.2d 129 (Conn. App. Ct. 1994).**

Find 708 N.W.2d 847 to answer Questions 8 and 9.

8.   State the full citation for 708 N.W.2d 847.

Our previous example of an intermediate state appellate court citation cited in a document submitted to a state court whose local rules also require citing to the official reporter would look like this. **Example:** *Maluszewski v. Allstate Ins. Co.,* **34 Conn. App. 27, 640 A.2d 129 (1994).**

9.   State the full citation for 708 N.W.2d 847, assuming you are including this citation in a document to a Nebraska state court whose local rules also require citing to the official report volume.

You should be aware that not all appellate court decisions are designated to be published by the issuing court. These cases are called **"unpublished"** or **"unreported"** cases. Historically, an attorney was not permitted to cite to an unpublished case except in very limited circumstances. However in recent years, some jurisdictions have amended their court rules to allow citing unpublished cases. For example, the Federal Rules of Appellate Procedure provide that a court must allow the citation of any unpublished federal opinion issued on or after Jan. 1, 2007 (FRAP 32.1). Check your federal circuit's local court rules to determine if opinions issued before Jan. 1, 2007 may be cited. In addition, you should check your state's court rules and determine whether or not you are permitted to cite to unreported state cases in state court.

Typically, unpublished cases can be found on the court's own Internet page as well as on Westlaw and Lexis Advance.

You want to find an unpublished case from the United States Court of Appeals, Fifth Circuit. **Go to the Fifth Circuit's site at http://www.ca5.uscourts.gov.**

10.   Search for the 2013 United States Court of Appeals, Fifth Circuit unpublished opinion with docket number 11-40750. Provide the proper citation to this exact copy (PDF) according to Rule 18.2.1 and Rule 10.8.1.

ASSIGNMENT ONE
FINDING AND CITING CASES
EXERCISE C

GOALS OF THIS ASSIGNMENT:
To teach you how to find cases on Westlaw when you have citations.
To familiarize you with the rules for citing cases in *The Bluebook: A Uniform System of Citation*, 20th ed.

CITATION RULES: Read the *Introduction*, Bluepages B10.1-B10.1.4, Rules 10.1-10.5, Bluepages B6, Rule 6.1, Rule 18.3, and Rule 10.8.1. Refer to Bluepages table BT2 and tables T1, T6, and T10.1 of *The Bluebook*. Apply these rules as you construct the correct citation for each case.

Throughout this book, when we ask that you provide a full citation to a case, give the name of the case, the published or unpublished source in which the case can be found, and a parenthetical indicating the court and year of decision as required by *The Bluebook*. Omit other parenthetical information and subsequent history unless you are told to include this information.

The first two questions introduce you to the rules for citing U.S. Supreme Court cases. **Example: *Loving v. Virginia*, 388 U.S. 1 (1967).**

United States Reports, abbreviated U.S. in case citations, is the official reporter. Note that no parallel, unofficial reporters are listed for U.S. Supreme Court cases when a U.S. citation is available. At the beginning of table T1.1 in *The Bluebook*, read the instructions for the **Supreme Court**.

1. If an opinion of the U.S. Supreme Court has not yet been published in *United States Reports*, which unofficial reporters should you cite instead, in order of preference?

Sign on to Westlaw.

2. Retrieve 526 U.S. 227 by citation. State the full citation for 526 U.S. 227.

The third question requires you to find and cite a U.S. Supreme Court case from before 1875. The reporters in which these cases were published are called **nominative** reporters, because they were generally known by the name of the person who compiled the volume. The form of citation for a case in a nominative reporter differs from the form for a case appearing in contemporary sources. Study the rules for citing cases found in nominative reporters (*The Bluebook* calls them "early American reporters." See Rule 10.3.2 and table T1.1.). Here is an example of how to cite an opinion in a U.S. Supreme Court nominative reporter: *Hughes v. Union Ins. Co.*, **21 U.S. (8 Wheat.) 294 (1823).**

Tip: For **accurate** dates of the United States Supreme Court nominative reporter decisions, **see http://www.supremecourt.gov/opinions/datesofdecisions.pdf**.

3.   Retrieve 77 U.S. 321 by citation. State the full citation for 77 U.S. 321.

Next, you must find and cite a federal court of appeals case from a circuit. When citing a court of appeals case, always list the circuit within the parentheses, along with the date. **Example: *Bonilla v. Volvo Car Corp.*, 150 F.3d 62 (1st Cir. 1998).**

4.   Retrieve 578 F.3d 823 by citation. State the full citation for 578 F.3d 823.

Now, find and cite a federal district court case. When citing a case from district court, the particular court is included within the parentheses. **Example: *Hillard v. Guidant Corp.*, 76 F. Supp. 2d 566 (M.D. Pa. 1999).**

5.   Retrieve 799 F. Supp. 2d 658 by citation. State the full citation for 799 F. Supp. 2d 658. **Note:** The district is listed before the state—the division, if listed, is listed after. Always include the district in the citation, never the division.

In general, for state decisions the state and the name of the court should be included within the parentheses. However, do not include the name of the court if the court of decision is the highest court of the state. Here is an example of how to cite a Pennsylvania Supreme Court case. How do you know what to include in the parentheses? Read Bluepages B10.1.3 and Rule 10.4(b) and look at the listing for Pennsylvania in table T1. **Example: *Commonwealth v. Brayboy*, 246 A.2d 675 (Pa. 1968).**

Retrieve 283 P.3d 904 by citation to answer Questions 6 and 7.

6.   State the full citation for 283 P.3d 904.

Should you ever cite the official version of a case? Yes, if the case is very old and there is no regional citation. Otherwise, you should cite it **only** if you are **including it in a document submitted to a state court whose local rules require citation to the official reporter.** (See Rule 10.3.1(a), Bluepages B10.1.3, and Bluepages table BT2.) Here is our previous example cited in such a context. **Example: *Commonwealth v. Brayboy,* 431 Pa. 365, 246 A.2d 675 (1968).** Note: We followed Rule 10.4(b) and omitted the jurisdiction Pa. from the parentheses because it is unambiguously conveyed by the reporter title.

7.   State the full citation for 283 P.3d 904, assuming you are including this citation in a document submitted to a state court whose local rules also require citing to the official report volume, if available, followed by the West reporter citation.

Next, find an opinion from a state intermediate appellate court and cite it correctly. **Example: *Maluszewski v. Allstate Ins. Co.,* 640 A.2d 129 (Conn. App. Ct. 1994).**

Retrieve 944 N.E.2d 172 by citation to answer Questions 8 and 9.

8.   State the full citation for 944 N.E.2d 172.

Our previous example of an intermediate state appellate court citation cited in a document submitted to a state court whose local rules also require citing to the official reporter would look like this. **Example: *Maluszewski v. Allstate Ins. Co.*, 34 Conn. App. 27, 640 A.2d 129 (1994).**

9.   State the full citation for 944 N.E.2d 172, assuming you are including this citation in a document to a Massachusetts state court whose local rules also require citing to the official report volume.

You should be aware that not all appellate court decisions are designated to be published by the issuing court. These cases are called **"unpublished"** or **"unreported"** cases. Historically, an attorney was not permitted to cite to an unpublished case except in very limited circumstances. However in recent years, some jurisdictions have amended their court rules to allow citing unpublished cases. For example, the Federal Rules of Appellate Procedure provide that a court must allow the citation of any unpublished federal opinion issued on or after Jan. 1, 2007 (FRAP 32.1). Check your federal circuit's local court rules to determine if opinions issued before Jan. 1, 2007 may be cited. In addition, you should check your state's court rules and determine whether or not you are permitted to cite to unreported state cases in state court.

Typically, unpublished cases can be found on the court's own Internet page as well as on Westlaw and Lexis Advance.

Slip opinions and unreported decisions may be retrieved by their unique Westlaw document number. Each case is assigned a Westlaw document number when it is loaded onto Westlaw. You can use this Westlaw document number as the citation when retrieving an unreported opinion by citation.

10.   Retrieve the 2012 United States Court of Appeals, Sixth Circuit opinion with Westlaw document number 2012 WL 6822056. Provide the proper citation according to Rule 18.3 and Rule 10.8.1.

ASSIGNMENT ONE
FINDING AND CITING CASES
EXERCISE D

GOALS OF THIS ASSIGNMENT:
To teach you how to find cases on Lexis Advance when you have citations.
To familiarize you with the rules for citing cases in *The Bluebook: A Uniform System of Citation*, 20th ed.

CITATION RULES: Read the *Introduction*, Bluepages B10.1-B10.1.4, Rules 10.1-10.5, Bluepages B6, Rule 6.1, Rule 18.3, and Rule 10.8.1. Refer to Bluepages table BT2 and tables T1, T6, and T10.1 of *The Bluebook*. Apply these rules as you construct the correct citation for each case.

Throughout this book, when we ask that you provide a full citation to a case, give the name of the case, the published or unpublished source in which the case can be found, and a parenthetical indicating the court and year of decision as required by *The Bluebook*. Omit other parenthetical information and subsequent history unless you are told to include this information.

The first two questions introduce you to the rules for citing U.S. Supreme Court cases. **Example: *Loving v. Virginia*, 388 U.S. 1 (1967).**

United States Reports, abbreviated U.S. in case citations, is the official reporter. Note that no parallel, unofficial reporters are listed for U.S. Supreme Court cases when a U.S. citation is available. At the beginning of table T1.1 in *The Bluebook*, read the instructions for the **Supreme Court**.

1.   If an opinion of the U.S. Supreme Court has not yet been published in *United States Reports*, which unofficial reporters should you cite instead, in order of preference?

Sign on to Lexis Advance.

2.   Retrieve 547 U.S. 489 by citation. State the full citation for 547 U.S. 489.

The third question requires you to find and cite a U.S. Supreme Court case from before 1875. The reporters in which these cases were published are called **nominative** reporters, because they were generally known by the name of the person who compiled the volume. The form of citation for a case in a nominative reporter differs from the form for a case appearing in contemporary sources. Study the rules for citing cases found in nominative reporters (*The Bluebook* calls them "early American reporters." See Rule 10.3.2 and table T1.1.). Here is an example of how to cite an opinion in a U.S. Supreme Court nominative reporter: *Hughes v. Union Ins. Co.*, **21 U.S. (8 Wheat.) 294 (1823).**

Tip: For **accurate** dates of the United States Supreme Court nominative reporter decisions, **see http://www.supremecourt.gov/opinions/datesofdecisions.pdf.** This document will also help with the name of the reporter's editor.

3.   Retrieve 27 U.S. 201 by citation. State the full citation for 27 U.S. 201.

Next, you must find and cite a federal court of appeals case from a circuit. When citing a court of appeals case, always list the circuit within the parentheses, along with the date. **Example: *Bonilla v. Volvo Car Corp.*, 150 F.3d 62 (1st Cir. 1998).**

4.   Retrieve 201 F.3d 188 by citation. State the full citation for 201 F.3d 188.

Now, find and cite a federal district court case. When citing a case from district court, the particular court is included within the parentheses. **Example: *Hillard v. Guidant Corp.*, 76 F. Supp. 2d 566 (M.D. Pa. 1999).**

5.   Retrieve 827 F. Supp. 2d 964 by citation. State the full citation for 827 F. Supp. 2d 964. **Note:** The district is listed before the state—the division, if listed, is listed after. Always include the district in the citation, never the division.

In general, for state decisions the state and the name of the court should be included within the parentheses. However, do not include the name of the court if the court of decision is the highest court of the state. Here is an example of how to cite a Pennsylvania Supreme Court case. How do you know what to include in the parentheses? Read Bluepages B10.1.3 and Rule 10.4(b) and look at the listing for Pennsylvania in table T.1. **Example:** *Commonwealth v. Brayboy*, **246 A.2d 675 (Pa. 1968).**

Retrieve 267 P.3d 1230 by citation to answer Questions 6 and 7.

6.   State the full citation for 267 P.3d 1230.

Should you ever cite the official version of a case? Yes, if the case is very old and there is no regional citation. Otherwise, you should cite it **only** if you are **including it in a document submitted to a state court whose local rules require citation to the official reporter.** (See Rule 10.3.1(a), Bluepages B10.1.3, and Bluepages table BT2.) Here is our previous example cited in such a context. **Example:** *Commonwealth v. Brayboy,* **431 Pa. 365, 246 A.2d 675 (1968).** Note: We followed Rule 10.4(b) and omitted the jurisdiction Pa. from the parentheses because it is unambiguously conveyed by the reporter title.

7.   State the full citation for 267 P.3d 1230, assuming you are including this citation in a document submitted to a state court whose local rules also require citing to the official report volume, if available, followed by the West reporter citation.

Next, find an opinion from a state intermediate appellate court and cite it correctly. **Example:** *Maluszewski v. Allstate Ins. Co.*, **640 A.2d 129 (Conn. App. Ct. 1994).**

Retrieve 988 A.2d 530 by citation to answer Questions 8 and 9.

8.   State the full citation for 988 A.2d 530.

Our previous example of an intermediate state appellate court citation cited in a document submitted to a state court whose local rules also require citing to the official reporter would look like this. **Example: *Maluszewski v. Allstate Ins. Co.*, 34 Conn. App. 27, 640 A.2d 129 (1994).**

9.   State the full citation for 988 A.2d 530, assuming you are including this citation in a document to a Maryland state court whose local rules also require citing to the official report volume.

You should be aware that not all appellate court decisions are designated to be published by the issuing court. These cases are called **"unpublished"** or **"unreported"** cases. Historically, an attorney was not permitted to cite to an unpublished case except in very limited circumstances. However in recent years, some jurisdictions have amended their court rules to allow citing unpublished cases. For example, the Federal Rules of Appellate Procedure provide that a court must allow the citation of any unpublished federal opinion issued on or after Jan. 1, 2007 (FRAP 32.1). Check your federal circuit's local court rules to determine if opinions issued before Jan. 1, 2007 may be cited. In addition, you should check your state's court rules and determine whether or not you are permitted to cite to unreported state cases in state court.

Typically, unpublished cases can be found on the court's own Internet page as well as on Westlaw and Lexis Advance.

Slip opinions and unreported decisions may be retrieved by their unique LexisNexis document number. Each case is assigned a LexisNexis document number that takes the place of a reporter citation. You can use this LexisNexis document number as the citation when retrieving an unpublished or unreported opinion by citation.

10.   Retrieve the 1998 United States Court of Appeals, Seventh Circuit opinion with LexisNexis document number 1998 U.S. App. LEXIS 32626. Provide the proper citation according to Rule 18.3 and Rule 10.8.1.

ASSIGNMENT TWO
SUPREME COURT REPORTERS AND PARTS OF A CASE
EXERCISE A

GOALS OF THIS ASSIGNMENT:
To familiarize you with the parts of a case in three different reporters.
To introduce you to star paging.

CITATION RULES: Use *The Bluebook: A Uniform System of Citation*, 20th ed., Bluepages B10.1.1, B10.1.2, B10.1.3, Rules 10.2, 10.2.1, 10.2.2, 10.3.1, 10.3.2, 10.4, 10.5, and tables T1, T6, and T10.1. Use the format for court documents and legal memoranda and assume that the case citation appears in a citation as opposed to a textual sentence.

Locate 468 U.S. 897 to answer Questions 1-9.

1. Find 468 U.S. 897. This is the official reporter version of the case. What is the case name? Use correct form according to *The Bluebook* rules for case names.

2. On what date was the case decided?

3. What is the docket number of the case?

4. Which party is the respondent?

5. Which Justice wrote the opinion of the Court?

6. Which two Justices filed dissenting opinions?

7. What was the lower court cite of this case, on its way up to the Supreme Court? **Note**: You are looking for the cite to an F.2d case.

8. How did the Supreme Court act on the judgment of the court below?

9. Who argued the cause for the United States?

To answer Questions 10-17 you will need to compare the case from Question 1 in the two unofficial versions, S. Ct., L. Ed., of this opinion.

10. Find the appropriate book of vol. 104 of the *Supreme Court Reporter* (S. Ct.), published by West, and vol. 82 of the *U.S. Supreme Court Reports--Lawyers' Edition* (L. Ed. 2d), whose volumes are currently published by LexisNexis. These two reporters are unofficial reporters for United States Supreme Court cases. Use the Cases Reported table at the front of S. Ct. and the Table of Cases Reported in the front of L. Ed. to find your case in both reporters.

    a. What is the S. Ct. cite?

    b. What is the L. Ed. 2d cite?

11. Examine the headnotes preceding the opinions. On which page of which reporter does the fourteenth West topic and key number appear? **Note**: A small key-shaped symbol accompanies the West topic and key number.

12.   State the West topic and key number from the preceding question.

13.   Each headnote corresponds to a particular part of the Court's opinion. Examine the opinion in S. Ct. and look for references to the headnote numbers (boldface numbers in brackets [1]). On which page of the S. Ct. **opinion** is there a reference to the fourteenth West headnote?

14.   Star paging enables attorneys using L. Ed. or S. Ct. to cite U.S. paging without having U.S. itself. Star paging in L. Ed. is shown thus: **[405 US 729]**. Star paging in S. Ct. is indicated thus: ⊥**729**. Looking at the *Supreme Court Reporter* and using star paging ⊥, state the page of *United States Reports* (U.S.) on which the corresponding material related to the fourteenth **[14]** West headnote begins.

15.   Notice that the two unofficial reporters have different headnotes. How many headnotes are in the *U.S. Supreme Court Reports, Lawyers' Edition*?

16.   Question 8 asked you about the **disposition** of the case, that is, how the Supreme Court treated the judgment of the court below. The **holding** is another part of a case, the application of rules of law to the specific key facts in the case. Did the Court hold that the exclusionary rule does not prohibit the use in the prosecution's case in chief of evidence obtained by police officers acting in reasonable reliance on a search warrant issued by a neutral and detached magistrate even if that warrant is ultimately found to be invalid? You may want to review the syllabus of the case.

17.   The exclusionary rule is a judicially created remedy for a violation of which Constitutional amendment as relevant to this opinion?

ASSIGNMENT TWO
SUPREME COURT REPORTERS AND PARTS OF A CASE
EXERCISE B

GOALS OF THIS ASSIGNMENT:
To familiarize you with the parts of a case in three different reporters.
To introduce you to star paging.

CITATION RULES: Use *The Bluebook: A Uniform System of Citation*, 20th ed., Bluepages B10.1.1, B10.1.2, B10.1.3, Rules 10.2, 10.2.1, 10.2.2, 10.3.1, 10.3.2, 10.4, 10.5, and tables T1, T6, and T10.1. Use the format for court documents and legal memoranda and assume that the case citation appears in a citation as opposed to a textual sentence.

Locate 476 U.S. 593 to answer Questions 1-9.

1. Find 476 U.S. 593. This is the official reporter version of the case. What is the case name? Use correct form according to *The Bluebook* rules for case names.

2. On what date was the case decided?

3. What is the docket number of the case?

4. Which party is the respondent?

5. Which Justice wrote the opinion of the Court?

6. Which Justice filed a dissenting opinion?

7.   What was the lower court cite of this case, on its way up to the Supreme Court? **Note**: You are looking for the cite to an F.2d case.

8.   How did the Supreme Court act on the judgment of the court below?

9.   Who argued the cause for the United States?

        To answer Questions 10-17, you will need to compare the case from Question 1 in the two unofficial versions, S. Ct., L. Ed., of this opinion.

10.   Find the appropriate book of vol. 106 of the *Supreme Court Reporter* (S. Ct.), published by West, and vol. 90 of the *U.S. Supreme Court Reports—Lawyers' Edition* (L. Ed. 2d), whose volumes are currently published by LexisNexis. These two reporters are unofficial reporters for United States Supreme Court cases. Use the Cases Reported table at the front of S. Ct. and the Table of Cases Reported in the front of L. Ed. to find your case in both reporters.

        a.   What is the S. Ct. cite?

        b.   What is the L. Ed. 2d cite?

11.   Examine the headnotes preceding the opinions. On what page of which reporter does the third West topic and key number appear? **Note**: A small key-shaped symbol accompanies the West topic and key number.

12.   State the West topic and key number from the preceding question.

13.   Each headnote corresponds to a particular part of the Court's opinion. Examine the opinion in S. Ct. and look for references to the headnote numbers (boldface numbers in brackets **[1]**). On what page of the S. Ct. **opinion** is there a reference to the third West headnote?

14.   Star paging enables attorneys using L. Ed. or S. Ct. to cite U.S. paging without using U.S. itself. Star paging in L. Ed. is shown thus: **[405 US 729]**. Star paging in S. Ct. is indicated thus: ⊥**729.** Looking at the *Supreme Court Reporter* and using star paging ⊥, state the page of *United States Reports* (U.S.) on which the corresponding material related to the third **[3]** West headnote begins.

15.   Notice that the two unofficial reporters have different headnotes. How many headnotes are in the *U.S. Supreme Court Reports, Lawyers' Edition*?

16.   Question 8 asked you about the **disposition** of the case, that is, how the Supreme Court treated the judgment of the court below. The **holding** is another part of a case, the application of rules of law to the specific key facts in the case. Did the Court hold that Hughes Properties, Inc. was entitled to claim the deductions as business expenses amounts guaranteed for payment on "progressive" slot machines but not yet won by playing patrons?

17.   On its federal income tax returns for certain fiscal years, Hughes Properties, Inc. claimed a deduction as an ordinary and necessary business expense incurred during the taxable year under what section of the Internal Revenue Code of 1954?

ASSIGNMENT TWO
SUPREME COURT REPORTERS AND PARTS OF A CASE
EXERCISE C

GOALS OF THIS ASSIGNMENT:
To familiarize you with the parts of a case on Westlaw.
To introduce you to star paging.

CITATION RULES: Use *The Bluebook: A Uniform System of Citation*, 20th ed., Bluepages B10.1.1, B10.1.2, B10.1.3, Rules 10.2, 10.2.1, 10.2.2, 10.3.1, 10.3.2, 10.4, 10.5, and tables T1, T6, and T10.1. Use the format for court documents and legal memoranda and assume that the case citation appears in a citation as opposed to a textual sentence.

Sign on to Westlaw and retrieve 523 U.S. 224 by citation.

1.   What is the case name? Use correct form according to *The Bluebook* rules for case names.

2.   On what date was the case decided?

3.   What is the docket number of the case?

4.   Which party is the petitioner?

5.   Which Justice wrote the opinion of the Court?

6.   Which Justice filed a dissenting opinion?

7.   What was the lower appellate court cite of this case, on its way up to the Supreme Court? **Note**: You are looking for the cite of an F.3d case.

8.   How did the Supreme Court act on the judgment of the court below?

9.   Who argued the cause for the petitioner?

10.   You found this case on Westlaw using its official *United States Reports* cite. Notice that Westlaw provides you with the citations to several other unofficial versions including the *Supreme Court Reporter* (S. Ct.), published by West, and the *U.S. Supreme Court Reports—Lawyers' Edition* (L. Ed. 2d), published by LexisNexis. These two reporters are unofficial reporters for United States Supreme Court cases.

   a.   What is the S. Ct. cite?

   b.   What is the L. Ed. 2d cite?

11.   The West editors add headnotes to the beginning of each case. The editors write a headnote, or summary, for each point of law in the case. Examine the headnotes preceding the opinion. How many headnotes have the West editors written for this case?

12.   The West editors assign at least one West topic and key number to each headnote. State the West topic name and key number assigned to headnote thirteen.
   Tip: If the headnotes are not displayed, click on the West Headnotes header. If the key number classification hierarchy is not displayed next to your headnote, click on **Change View**. The topic is the first line of the hierarchy and your key number will be in the last line.

13.   Each headnote is a summary of a point of law from the Court's opinion. Since the headnote is written by a West editor and not a member of the Court, you cannot cite the language of the headnote as precedent. You must cite the language written by the justice in the opinion. Link to or scroll to the part of the opinion where the point of law from headnote thirteen is discussed. Read the section. Does the doctrine of "constitutional doubt" apply mechanically whenever there is not an obvious answer to a significant constitutional question?

14.   *The Bluebook* requires citing an opinion of the United States Supreme Court to the official reports (U.S.), if available. Star paging enables attorneys using Westlaw to cite to the *United States Reports* (U.S.) paging without using U.S. itself. On Westlaw, page numbers preceded by one asterisk indicate the *United States Reports* (U.S.) pages and page numbers preceded by two asterisks indicate *Supreme Court Reporter* (S. Ct.) pages. Looking at the case on Westlaw and using star paging, state the page of *United States Reports* (U.S.) on which the opinion's text begins discussing the point of law found in West headnote thirteen **[13]**. **Hint**: You may need to scroll up until you see the number preceded by one asterisk.

15.   On what page of the *Supreme Court Reporter* (S. Ct.) do you find the opinion's text that discusses the point of law from the thirteenth **[13]** West headnote? **Hint**: Remember to use the asterisks as your guide.

16.   Question 8 asked you about the **disposition** of the case, that is, how the Supreme Court treated the judgment of the court below. The **holding** is another part of a case, the application of rules of law to the specific key facts in the case. Did the Court hold that a statutory subsection providing an enhanced sentence for any alien who illegally returned to the United States after being deported following a conviction of an aggravated felony created a separate immigration related offense? You may want to review the syllabus of the case.

17.   What federal statute makes it a crime for a deported alien to return to the United States without special permission and authorizes a maximum prison term of two years?

ASSIGNMENT TWO
SUPREME COURT REPORTERS AND PARTS OF A CASE
EXERCISE D

GOALS OF THIS ASSIGNMENT:
To familiarize you with the parts of a case on Lexis Advance.
To introduce you to star paging.

CITATION RULES: Use *The Bluebook: A Uniform System of Citation*, 20th ed., Bluepages B10.1.1, B10.1.2, B10.1.3, Rules 10.2, 10.2.1, 10.2.2, 10.3.1, 10.3.2, 10.4, 10.5, and tables T1, T6, and T10.1. Use the format for court documents and legal memoranda and assume that the case citation appears in a citation as opposed to a textual sentence.

Sign on to Lexis Advance and retrieve 535 U.S. 391 by citation.

1.   What is the case name? Use correct form according to *The Bluebook* rules for case names.

2.   On what date was the case decided?

3.   What is the docket number of the case?

4.   Which party is the petitioner?

5.   Which Justice wrote the opinion of the court?

6.   Which two Justices filed dissenting opinions?

7.   What was the lower appellate court cite of this case, on its way up to the Supreme Court? **Note**: You are looking for the cite of an F.3d case.

8.   How did the Supreme Court act on the judgment of the court below?

9.   Who argued the cause for the petitioner?

10.   You found this case on Lexis Advance using its official *United States Reports* cite. Notice that Lexis Advance provides you with the citations to several other unofficial versions including the *Supreme Court Reporter* (S. Ct.), published by West, and the *U.S. Supreme Court Reports–Lawyers' Edition* (L. Ed. 2d), published by LexisNexis. These two reporters are unofficial reporters for United States Supreme Court cases.

       a.   What is the S. Ct. cite?

       b.   What is the L. Ed. 2d cite?

11.   The LexisNexis editors add headnotes to the beginning of each case. The editors write a headnote, or summary, for each key legal point of a case. In addition, you will see the headnotes that editors wrote for the print version found in *U.S. Supreme Court Reports–Lawyers' Edition*. How many LexisNexis headnotes have the editors written for this case?

12.   The LexisNexis editors assign topics to each headnote. State the complete topic from LexisNexis headnote ten, including the levels of the topic hierarchy which begins with a broad practice area as shown in the case.

13.   Each headnote is a summary of a key legal point of the Court's opinion. Since the headnote is written by a LexisNexis editor and not a member of the Court, you cannot cite the language of the headnote as precedent. You must cite the language written by the justice in the opinion. Link or scroll to the part of the opinion where the point of law from headnote ten is discussed. Read the section. Does the American with Disabilities Act of 1990 ordinarily require an employer to assign a disabled employee to a particular position even though another employee is entitled to that position under the employee's established seniority system?

14.   *The Bluebook* requires citing an opinion of the United States Supreme Court to the official reports (U.S.), if available. Star paging enables attorneys using Lexis Advance to cite to the *United States Reports* (U.S.) paging without using U.S. itself. Looking at the case on Lexis Advance and using star paging, state the page of *United States Reports* (U.S.) on which the opinion's text begins discussing the point of law found in LexisNexis headnote ten **[HN10]**.

        Tip: To view a specific reporter version's pagination, click on the reporter citation in the list of parallel cites under **Reporter** at the top of the opinion. Page numbers are indicated by bold bracketed numbers in the opinion. Remember that you may need to scroll up slightly to see the bold bracketed page number for your text.

15.   On what page of the *Supreme Court Reporter* (S. Ct.) do you find the opinion's text that discusses the point of law from the tenth **[HN10]** LexisNexis headnote?

16.   Question 8 asked you about the **disposition** of the case, that is, how the Supreme Court treated the judgment of the court below. The **holding** is another part of a case, the application of rules of law to the specific key facts in the case. Did the Court hold an employer's showing that a requested accommodation conflicts with seniority rules is ordinarily sufficient to show, as a matter of law, that an accommodation is not reasonable? You may want to review the syllabus of the case.

17.   Where in the United States Code can you find the Americans with Disabilities Act of 1990 codified?

ASSIGNMENT THREE
REGIONAL REPORTER CASES
EXERCISE A

GOALS OF THIS ASSIGNMENT:
To acquaint you with the Table of Cases in the digests.
To compare the features of regional reporters.

CITATION RULES: For this assignment when citing a case, assume you are citing the case in a legal document that will be submitted to a state court that does not require parallel cites.

Assume you want to find the unofficial (West reporter or regional reporter) text of *Rewolinski v. Harley-Davidson Motor Co.*, a 1966 Supreme Court of Wisconsin case. When you know the case name and jurisdiction, but do not know the citation, one way to find the citation is to look it up in a digest's table of cases. Look up *Rewolinski v. Harley-Davidson Motor Co.* in the Table of Cases volume in *West's Wisconsin Key Number Digest*, the *North Western Digest 2d*, or the *Eighth Decennial Digest*.

1. What is the full citation of the case? (Remember, this means name, cite to the reporter, jurisdiction, court, and year according to Bluepages B10 and Rule 10 of *The Bluebook*.)

Find the unofficial report of the case in the *North Western Reporter* and answer Questions 2-8.

2. Notice the one-paragraph summary of the facts and holding at the beginning of the case. This is called the synopsis and West editors wrote it. According to the synopsis, how did the Supreme Court dispose of the decision of the Circuit Court?

3. Notice the headnotes (one-sentence summaries of points of law). All headnotes in the regional reporters that follow West topic and key numbers are written by West editors. How many headnotes are listed here?

4. A topic and key number precede each headnote in a regional reporter, like those you saw in Assignment Two. What is the topic and key number for the third headnote?

Never quote from or cite to the synopsis or headnotes. You must cite to the actual opinion. You can, however, search them on Westlaw, along with the topics and key numbers. Cases are divided into different parts, called **fields** on Westlaw and **segments** on Lexis Advance. Fields and segments can be searched separately, or with the rest of the case.

5. Remember, you can find the part of the opinion that corresponds to the third headnote by looking for the corresponding boldface number in brackets in the opinion. On what page of the opinion do you find the corresponding text for the third headnote?

6. Read the opinion. Did the court state that it had the authority to overturn a jury's apportionment of negligence in safe-place cases?

7. Look at the beginning of the case. What is the cite to the official reports citation, which is given just above the name of the case?

8. Look at the title page of the *North Western Reporter* volume. List **five** states covered in the *North Western Reporter*.

9. Using your textbook or *The Bluebook: A Uniform System of Citation*, state the regional reporters in which the following states' cases are found:

    a. Alabama

    b. Delaware

    c. New Mexico

In this assignment, you used the table of cases in a digest to find the cite to a case. You then found that case in a regional reporter. Does your own state have an official reporter or public domain citation format? Check table T1 in *The Bluebook* or ask your instructor.

ASSIGNMENT THREE
REGIONAL REPORTER CASES
EXERCISE B

GOALS OF THIS ASSIGNMENT:
To acquaint you with the Table of Cases in the digests.
To compare the features of regional reporters.

CITATION RULES: For this assignment when citing a case, assume you are citing the case in a legal document that will be submitted to a state court that does not require parallel cites.

Assume you want to find the unofficial (West reporter or regional reporter) text of *Blanchard v. Gilmore*, a 1952 Supreme Court of Georgia case. When you know the case name and jurisdiction, but do not know the citation, one way to find the citation is to look it up in a digest's table of cases. Look up *Blanchard v. Gilmore* in the Table of Cases volume in the *Georgia Digest 2d*, the *South Eastern Digest 2d*, or the *Sixth Decennial Digest*.

1. What is the full citation of the case? (Remember, this means name, cite to the reporter, jurisdiction, court, and year according to Bluepages B10 and Rule 10 of *The Bluebook*.)

Find the unofficial report of the case in the *South Eastern Reporter* and answer Questions 2-8.

2. Notice the one-paragraph summary of the facts and holding at the beginning of the case. This is called the synopsis and West editors wrote it. According to the synopsis, how did the Supreme Court dispose of the decision of the Superior Court?

3. Notice the headnotes (one-sentence summaries of points of law). All headnotes in the regional reporters that follow West topic and key numbers are written by West editors. How many headnotes are listed here?

4. A topic and key number precede each headnote in a regional reporter, like those you saw in Assignment Two. What is the topic and key number for the fourth headnote?

Never quote from or cite to the synopsis or headnotes. You must cite to the actual opinion. You can, however, search them on Westlaw, along with the topics and key numbers. Cases are divided into different parts, called **fields** on Westlaw and **segments** on Lexis Advance. Fields and segments can be searched separately, or with the rest of the case.

5.   Remember, you can find the part of the opinion that corresponds to the fourth headnote by looking for the corresponding boldface number in brackets in the opinion. On what page of the opinion do you find the corresponding text for the fourth headnote?

6.   Read the opinion. Did the court hold that the trustees should deliver the corpus of the estate to Thomas W. Gilmore Jr., subject to the corpus being charged with the rights of the wife as stated in the will?

7.   Look at the beginning of the case. What is the citation to the official reports, which is given just above the name of the case?

8.   Look at the title page of a *South Eastern Reporter* volume. List the **five** states covered in the *South Eastern Reporter*.

9.   Using your textbook or *The Bluebook: A Uniform System of Citation*, state the regional reporters in which the following states' cases are found:

          a. Colorado

          b. Iowa

          c. Tennessee

In this assignment, you used the table of cases in a digest to find the cite to a case. You then found that case in a regional reporter. Does your own state have an official reporter or public domain citation format? Check table T1 in *The Bluebook* or ask your instructor.

ASSIGNMENT THREE
REGIONAL REPORTER CASES
EXERCISE C

GOALS OF THIS ASSIGNMENT:
To acquaint you with retrieving a case by name on Westlaw.
To compare the features of regional reporters.

CITATION RULES: For this assignment when citing a case, assume you are citing the case in a legal document that will be submitted to a state court that does not require parallel cites.

Sign on to Westlaw.

Assume you want to find the unofficial (West reporter or regional reporter) text of *Gomes v. Commercial Union Insurance Co.*, a 2001 Supreme Court of Connecticut case. When you know the case name and jurisdiction but do not know the citation, one way to find the citation is to use the Title field search with the appropriate jurisdiction on Westlaw to search only the names of the cases. For example, the search **TI(Smith & Jones)** will pull up all cases in the selected jurisdiction where the name contains both Smith and Jones. Use the Title field search and retrieve *Gomes v. Commercial Union Insurance Co.* **Note**: This search is parallel to using a print digest's Table of Cases to find the citation to a case when you know only the name of the case.

1. What is the full citation of the case? (Remember, this means name, cite to the reporter, jurisdiction, court, and year according to Bluepages B10 and Rule 10 of *The Bluebook*.) Select the jurisdiction before you search.

Scroll through the unofficial report of the case from the *Atlantic Reporter 2d* on Westlaw and answer Questions 2-8.

2. Notice the short summary paragraph that gives the background and holding at the beginning of the opinion. This is called the synopsis and West editors wrote it. According to the synopsis, how did the Supreme Court dispose of the decision of the Superior Court?

3.   Notice the headnotes (one-sentence summaries of points of law). All headnotes in the regional reporters that follow West topic and key numbers are written by West editors. How many headnotes are listed here?

4.   A topic and key number precede each headnote in a published case on Westlaw, like those you saw in Assignment Two. What is the topic and key number for the second headnote?
      Tip: If the headnotes are not displayed, click on the West Headnotes header. If the key number classification hierarchy is not displayed next to your headnote, click on **Change View**. The topic is the first line of the hierarchy and your key number will be in the last line.

      Never quote from or cite to the synopsis or headnotes. You must cite to the actual opinion. You can, however, search them on Westlaw, along with the topics and key numbers.

      Cases are divided into different parts, called **fields** on Westlaw. You can run a search in a jurisdiction where you limit the search to look only at the fields of a case that you specify instead of the entire test of the case. You can search the synopsis using the synopsis (**SY**) field, the digest topic and key number using the topic (**TO**) field, the headnote summary paragraph using the headnote (**HE**) field, and both the topic and headnote using the digest (**DI**) field.

5.   Remember, you can link to the part of the opinion that corresponds to the second headnote by clicking on the bracketed headnote number. On what page of the *Atlantic Reporter 2d* version of the opinion do you find the corresponding text for the second headnote? Remember star paging from Assignment Two. **Hint:** Remember to use the asterisks as your guide.

6.   Read the opinion. What is the cite to the Connecticut Unfair Trade Practices Act?

7.   Look at the beginning of the case. What is the official cite, which is given in the header as well as at the beginning of the case?

8.   One of the nice features included in cases on Westlaw that is not included in the reporter version is the ability to see what subtopic the key number represents. Look at headnote two. What subtopic under topic "Innkeepers" does key number 14.1 stand for?
        Tip: If the headnotes are not displayed, click on the West Headnotes header. If the key number classification hierarchy is not displayed next to your headnote, click on **Change View**.

9.   Using you textbook or *The Bluebook: A Uniform System of Citation*, state the regional reporters in which the following states' cases are found:

                a. Connecticut

                b. Indiana

                c. Oregon

        In this assignment, you retrieved a case by party name on Westlaw since you knew the case name and its jurisdiction. Does your own state have an official reporter or a public domain citation format? Check table T1 in *The Bluebook* or ask your instructor.

ASSIGNMENT THREE
REGIONAL REPORTER CASES
EXERCISE D

GOALS OF THIS ASSIGNMENT:
To acquaint you with the Name segment search on Lexis Advance.
To compare the features of regional reporters.

CITATION RULES: For this assignment when citing a case, assume you are citing the case in a legal document that will be submitted to a state court that does not require parallel cites.

Sign on to Lexis Advance.

Assume you want to find the unofficial (West reporter or regional reporter) text of *Barnett v. Hawk Pharmacy, Inc.*, a 1976 Supreme Court of Kansas case. When you know the case name and jurisdiction but do not know the citation, use the Name segment search on Lexis Advance to search only the names of cases. For example, the search **NAME(Smith & Jones)** will pull up all cases in the jurisdiction where the name contains both Smith and Jones. Use the Name segment search and retrieve *Barnett v. Hawk Pharmacy, Inc.* **Note**: This search is parallel to using a print digest's Table of Cases to find the citation to a case when you know only the name of the case.

1.   What is the full citation of the case? (Remember, this means name, cite to the reporter, jurisdiction, court and year according to Bluepages B10 and Rule 10 of *The Bluebook*.) Set your filters before you search.

Scroll through the case on Lexis Advance and answer Questions 2-8.

2.   Notice the **Case Summary** box. The case summary provides the procedural posture, overview, and outcome of the case. The case summary information is written by LexisNexis editors. According to the case summary, what was the outcome of the Supreme Court of Kansas case?

3.   Notice the headnotes (short summaries of points of law). LexisNexis headnotes are written by LexisNexis editors. How many headnotes are listed here?

4.   Each LexisNexis headnote is assigned at least one topic and sometimes more than one topic. What is the first topic for the second LexisNexis headnote?

Never quote from or cite to the case summary or headnotes. You must cite to the actual opinion. You can, however, search them on Lexis Advance.

Cases are divided into different parts, called **segments** on Lexis Advance. You can run a search in a jurisdiction's cases where you limit the search to look only at the segments of a case that you specify. To see the segments available, set your filters to any jurisdiction and cases as the category. Then click on Advanced Search to view the available segments.

Once you have found a case of interest, you can navigate to a particular point in the case by using the **Go to** feature on Lexis Advance. When you click on **Go to** a list of parts will display. Click on the part that you want to read. You are taken directly to that part of the case. You can select parts of the case including case summary, overview, outcome, and LexisNexis headnotes among others.

5.   Remember, you can link to the part of the opinion that corresponds to the second headnote by clicking on the headnote number. On what page of the *Pacific Reporter* version of the opinion do you find the corresponding text for the second headnote?
Tip: Change your Report view to the Pacific Reporter version and then click on the headnote number. Scroll up to see the bold bracketed page number.

6.   Read the opinion. Under a well-established rule in the jurisdiction, what should happen when there is ground for a strong suspicion that the jury awarded inadequate damages to the plaintiff as a result of a compromise involving the question of liability?

7. Look at the beginning of the case. What is the official cite, which is given in the header as well as at the beginning of the case?

8. Go back to the LexisNexis headnotes for the case. Look at the first topic for the second headnote. If you click on one of the topic links, are you able to view a topic index?

9. Using your textbook or *The Bluebook: A Uniform System of Citation*, state the regional reporters in which the following states' cases are found:

        a. Hawaii

        b. Michigan

        c. Pennsylvania

In this assignment, you retrieved a case by party name on Lexis Advance since you knew the case name and its jurisdiction. Does your own state have an official reporter or public domain citation format? Check table T1 in *The Bluebook* or ask your instructor.

ASSIGNMENT FOUR
FINDING CASES BY SUBJECT
EXERCISE A

GOALS OF THIS ASSIGNMENT:
To introduce you to finding cases by subject in the West digests.
To give you practice at the various methods of using digests.

CITATION RULES: For this assignment when citing a case, assume you are citing the case in a legal document that will be submitted to a state court that does not require parallel cites.

Please research federal cases for the Fifth Circuit. We are looking at federal crimes and double jeopardy. We need to confirm that when the same act or transaction is a violation of two distinct statutory provisions, the test to be applied to determine whether there are two offenses or only one for double jeopardy purposes, is whether each statutory provision requires proof of an additional element that the other does not. Another attorney has given you a relevant case, *United States v. Lankford*, a 1999 United States Court of Appeals, Fifth Circuit case which has a headnote on point. Use this case to find other relevant cases. This is called the "one good case" approach. Check the Table of Cases in either 1) the *West's Federal Practice Digest 4th* or 2) the *Eleventh Decennial Digest, Part 1* (in that order of preference) to find the West reporter cite for the case.

1.   What is the West reporter cite for the case?

2.   Look up the case in the West reporter. The relevant headnote for our issue is headnote twenty-six. What is the **first listed** West topic and key number of headnote twenty-six?

3.   We now have a West topic and key number to begin our digest research. First, let's find out just what this topic and key number represent. Find the analysis outline at the very beginning of the topic from Question 2 in your digest. Examine the list of key numbers. What does the key number from Question 2 stand for? Include all relevant topics of which your key number may be a subtopic.

You will be using the same digest to answer Questions 4-11a or 4-11b.

4.   Go to your key number and look at the cases listed under it. Is there another United States Court of Appeals, Fifth Circuit case arising out of Texas from 1998 digested under this topic and key number? If so, provide the full West reporter citation of the case according to Bluepages B10 and Rule 10 of *The Bluebook*.

5.   Now you will use the topic approach. The topic approach merely involves reading the list of key numbers at the beginning of the topic (the topic outline) and looking for relevant key numbers. Go back to the topic outline (called "Analysis") for **Double Jeopardy**. If you were looking for cases concerning the identity of particular offenses and specifically weapons offenses, under what topic and key number would you look?

6.   Look up that key number. State the name **as listed** of the 1997 United States Court of Appeals, Fifth Circuit case arising out of Texas that discusses the permissibility under double jeopardy of prosecuting for both possession of stolen firearm and possession of firearm with obliterated serial number.

7.   Now you will use the keyword approach. Look in the Descriptive Word Index volumes (either at the beginning or the end of the set). Using the descriptive word approach, find the topic and key number for cases dealing with attachment of jeopardy when there is a directed verdict. To what topic and key number are you referred?

8.   Look up the topic and key number and find a 1996 United States Court of Appeals, Fifth Circuit case arising out of Texas. List the full West reporter citation of the case in correct form without subsequent history.

SECTION I: Complete Questions 9a-13a in Section I if you used *West's Federal Practice Digest 4th* for this assignment.

HOW TO UPDATE YOUR DIGEST RESEARCH IF YOU ARE USING *WEST'S FEDERAL PRACTICE DIGEST 4TH*:

Step 1.   Current digest volumes are supplemented by annual pocket parts. Look in the pocket part for your topic and key number.
    OR
If the pocket part is too thick to fit in the volume, the pocket part becomes a free standing pamphlet that updates that particular volume. Look in the pamphlet for your topic and key number.

Step 2.   Depending on how recently the annual pocket parts were issued, your digest may have a pamphlet that directly supplements the annual pocket parts. If so, look up your topic and key number in this pamphlet.

Step 3.   If the digest has a supplemental pamphlet from Step 2, check the "Closing with Cases Reported in" section on the second page of the pamphlet. If there is not a supplemental pamphlet, check the "Closing with Cases Reported in" section on the second page of the pocket part/pamphlet from Step 1. Note the closing reporter.

Step 4.   Go the reporter volume that you identified in Step 3. Beginning with the volume listed in the "Closing with Cases Reported in" from Step 3, look in the digest sections in the back of all bound volumes and in the front of all advance sheets to see if any recent cases have appeared under your topic and key number.

9a.   Does your digest volume have a pocket part or pamphlet as explained in Step 1? If so, look up the topic and key number from Question 7. Are there any cases from the United States Court of Appeals, Fifth Circuit digested under this topic and key number?

10a.   Does your digest have a supplemental pamphlet as explained in Step 2? If so, look up the topic and key number from Question 7. Are there any cases from the United States Court of Appeals, Fifth Circuit digested under this topic and key number?

11a.   Perform Step 3 of updating the digest by looking at the "Closing with Cases Reported in" statement on the second page of the supplemental pamphlet for the digest if there are any. If not, look at the "Closing with Cases Reported in" on the second page of the pocket part/pamphlet. According to the "Closing with Cases Reported in," what is the last volume of F.3d that the digest pocket part/pamphlet covers?

Now go to the *Federal Reporter 3d* and find the volume from Question 11a.

12a.   Each bound reporter volume has a small digest section in the back which gives you the topics and key numbers for the cases printed in that volume. Normally, you would check the digest sections of all of the bound reporters on the shelf beginning with the volume from Question 11a. For this assignment, however, check **only** the **most recent** bound volume. Are there any United States Court of Appeals, Fifth Circuit cases digested under your topic and key number?

13a.   Now check the *Federal Reporter's* advance sheets. Bound volumes are updated by paperbound advance sheets. Several advance sheets are bound together into a reporter. In advance sheets, the digest section is in the front, just before the decisions begin. Normally, you would look at the digest section in all of the advance sheets for your topic and key number. For this assignment, however, check **only** the **most recent** advance sheet. Are there any United States Court of Appeals, Fifth Circuit cases are digested under your topic and key number?

SECTION II: Complete Questions 9b-13b in Section II if you used a Decennial Digest for this assignment.

HOW TO UPDATE YOUR DIGEST RESEARCH IF YOU ARE USING A DECENNIAL DIGEST:

Step 1.   Look for your topic and key number in all of the subsequent Decennial Digests that were issued after the one you used in this assignment.

Step 2.   The most recent Decennial Digest is updated by the General Digest. You will need to look at every volume of the General Digest for your topic and key number.

Step 3. Check the "Closing with Cases Reported in" on the second page of the last General Digest on the shelf. Note the closing reporter.

Step 4. Go the reporter volume that you identified in Step 3. Beginning with the volume listed in the "Closing with Cases Reported in" from Step 3, look in the digest sections in the back of all bound volumes and in the front of all advance sheets to see if any recent cases have appeared under your topic and key number.

9b. Are there any subsequent Decennial Digests since the Decennial Digest you used in this exercise? If so, look up the topic and key number from Question 7 in each subsequent Decennial Digest. Are there any cases from the United States Court of Appeals, Fifth Circuit digested under this topic and key number?

10b. Find the General Digests. Look up the topic and key number from Question 7 in each volume of the General Digest. Are there any cases from the United States Court of Appeals, Fifth Circuit digested under this topic and key number?

11b. Perform Step 3 of updating the digest by looking at the "Closing with Cases Reported in" statement on the second page of the last General Digest on the shelf. According to the "Closing with Cases Reported in," what is the last volume of F.3d that this volume of the General Digest covers?

Now go to the *Federal Reporter 3d* and find the volume from Question 11b.

12b. Each bound reporter volume has a small digest section in the back which gives you the topics and key numbers for the cases printed in that volume. Normally, you would check the digest sections of all of the bound reporters on the shelf beginning with the volume from Question 11b. For this assignment, however, check **only** the **most recent** bound volume. Are there any United States Court of Appeals, Fifth Circuit cases digested under your topic and key number?

13b.   Now check the *Federal Reporter's* advance sheets. Bound volumes are updated by paperbound advance sheets. Several advance sheets are bound together into a reporter. In advance sheets, the digest section is in the front, just before the decisions begin. Normally, you would look at the digest section in all of the advance sheets for your topic and key number. For this assignment, however, check **only** the **most recent** advance sheet. Are there any United States Court of Appeals, Fifth Circuit cases digested under your topic and key number?

One great advantage of the West topic and key number system is that you can use it for **all jurisdictions**. The same topic and key number for a specific point of law can be used for researching all state and federal courts whose decisions are published in West reporters. Different West digests will group jurisdictions in different ways.

Regional digests contain state cases from each state covered by that particular region. The federal digests cover all of the federal courts, and the Decennial and General Digests, all of the state and federal jurisdictions. Use the most appropriate digest in your library, and provide the full citation, in correct form, for the following case. Search under the topic and key number from **Question 2**.

14.   Check *West's California Digest 2d* or the *Eleventh Decennial Digest, Part 1*. Provide the full West's California Reporter citation, in correct form, of the 1997 California Court of Appeal case digested under the topic and key number from Question 2.

ASSIGNMENT FOUR
FINDING CASES BY SUBJECT
EXERCISE B

GOALS OF THIS ASSIGNMENT:
To introduce you to finding cases by subject in the West digests.
To give you practice at the various methods of using digests.

CITATION RULES: For this assignment when citing a case, assume you are citing the case in a legal document that will be submitted to a state court that does not require parallel cites.

Please research federal cases for the Seventh Circuit. We need to research the federal law of conspiracy to determine if the government must prove knowing participation to prove conspiracy or if mere association with conspirators is enough. Another attorney has given you a relevant case, *United States v. Paiz,* a 1990 United States Court of Appeals, Seventh Circuit case which has a headnote on point. Use this case to find other relevant cases. This is called the "one good case" approach. Check the Table of Cases in either 1) the *West's Federal Practice Digest 4th* or 2) the *Tenth Decennial Digest, Part 1* (in that order of preference) to find the West reporter cite for the case.

1.   What is the West reporter cite for the case?

2.   Look up the case in the West reporter. The relevant headnote for our issue is headnote two. What is the West topic and key number of headnote two?

3.   We now have a West topic and key number to begin our digest research. First, let's find out just what this topic and key number represent. Find the analysis outline at the very beginning of the topic from Question 2 in your digest. Examine the list of key numbers. What does the key number from Question 2 stand for? Include all relevant topics of which your key number may be a subtopic.

You will be using the same digest to answer Questions 4-11a or 4-11b.

4. Go to your key number and look at the cases listed under it. Is there a United States Court of Appeals, Seventh Circuit case arising out of Indiana from 1986 digested under this topic and key number? If so, provide the full West reporter citation of the case according to Bluepages B10 and Rule 10 of *The Bluebook*.

5. Now you will use the topic approach. The topic approach merely involves reading the list of key numbers at the beginning of the topic (the topic outline) and looking for relevant key numbers. Go back to the topic outline (called "Analysis") for **Conspiracy**. If you were looking for cases that indicate the weight and sufficiency in general of evidence for the prosecution of criminal conspiracy, under what topic and key number would you look?

6. Look up that key number. State the name **as listed** of the 1989 United States Court of Appeals, Seventh Circuit case arising out of Indiana that indicates that once a conspiracy is shown to exist, evidence establishing defendant's participation beyond a reasonable doubt, even if connection between defendant and conspiracy is slight, is sufficient to convict.

7. Now you will use the keyword approach. Look in the Descriptive Word Index volumes (either at the beginning or the end of the set). Using the descriptive word approach, find the topic and key number for cases concerning the admissibility of evidence of predicate acts or overt acts in prosecution for criminal conspiracy?

8. Look up the topic and key number and find the 1987 United States Court of Appeals, Seventh Circuit case arising out of Indiana that states that accomplice testimony about numerous drug transactions involving the defendant was within the scope of alleged single conspiracy and thus admissible. List the full West reporter citation of the case in correct form.

SECTION I: Complete Questions 9a-13a in Section I if you used *West's Federal Practice Digest 4th* for this assignment.

HOW TO UPDATE YOUR DIGEST RESEARCH IF YOU ARE USING *WEST'S FEDERAL PRACTICE DIGEST 4TH*:

Step 1.   Current digest volumes are supplemented by annual pocket parts. Look in the pocket part for your topic and key number.
          OR
If the pocket part is too thick to fit in the volume, the pocket part becomes a free standing pamphlet that updates that particular volume. Look in the pamphlet for your topic and key number.

Step 2.   Depending on how recently the annual pocket parts were issued, your digest may have a pamphlet that directly supplements the annual pocket parts. If so, look up your topic and key number in this pamphlet.

Step 3.   If the digest has a supplemental pamphlet from Step 2, check the "Closing with Cases Reported in" section on the second page of the pamphlet. If there is not a supplemental pamphlet, check the "Closing with Cases Reported in" section on the second page of the pocket part/pamphlet from Step 1. Note the closing reporter.

Step 4.   Go the reporter volume that you identified in Step 3. Beginning with the volume listed in the "Closing with Cases Reported in" from Step 3, look in the digest sections in the back of all bound volumes and in the front of all advance sheets to see if any recent cases have appeared under your topic and key number.

9a.   Does your digest volume have a pocket part or pamphlet as explained in Step 1? If so, look up the topic and key number from Question 7. Are there any cases from the United States Court of Appeals, Seventh Circuit digested under this topic and key number?

10a.   Does your digest have a supplemental pamphlet as explained in Step 2? If so, look up the topic and key number from Question 7. Are there any cases from the United States Court of Appeals, Seventh Circuit digested under this topic and key number?

11a.   Perform Step 3 of updating the digest by looking at the "Closing with Cases Reported in" statement on the second page of the supplemental pamphlet for the digest if there are any. If not, look at the "Closing with Cases Reported in" on the second page of the pocket part/pamphlet. According to the "Closing with Cases Reported in," what is the last volume of F.3d that the digest pocket part/pamphlet covers?

Now go to the *Federal Reporter 3d* and find the volume from Question 11a.

12a.   Each bound reporter volume has a small digest section in the back which gives you the topics and key numbers for the cases printed in that volume. Normally, you would check the digest sections of all of the bound reporters on the shelf beginning with the volume from Question 11a. For this assignment, however, check **only** the **most recent** bound volume. Are there any United States Court of Appeals, Seventh Circuit cases digested under your topic and key number?

13a.   Now check the *Federal Reporter's* advance sheets. Bound volumes are updated by paperbound advance sheets. Several advance sheets are bound together into a reporter. In advance sheets, the digest section is in the front, just before the decisions begin. Normally, you would look at the digest section in all of the advance sheets for your topic and key number. For this assignment, however, check **only** the **most recent** advance sheet. Are there any United States Court of Appeals, Seventh Circuit cases are digested under your topic and key number?

SECTION II: Complete Questions 9b-13b in Section II if you used a Decennial Digest for this assignment.

HOW TO UPDATE YOUR DIGEST RESEARCH IF YOU ARE USING A DECENNIAL DIGEST:

Step 1.   **Look for your topic and key number in all of the subsequent Decennial Digests that were issued after the one you used in this assignment.**

Step 2.   **The most recent Decennial Digest is updated by the General Digest. You will need to look at every volume of the General Digest for your topic and key number.**

Step 3.   **Check the "Closing with Cases Reported in" on the second page of the last General Digest on the shelf. Note the closing reporter.**

Step 4.   **Go the reporter volume that you identified in Step 3. Beginning with the volume listed in the "Closing with Cases Reported in" from Step 3, look in the digest sections in the back of all bound volumes and in the front of all advance sheets to see if any recent cases have appeared under your topic and key number.**

9b.   Are there any subsequent Decennial Digests since the Decennial Digest you used in this exercise? If so, look up the topic and key number from Question 7 in each subsequent Decennial Digest. Are there any cases from the United States Court of Appeals, Seventh Circuit digested under this topic and key number?

10b.   Find the General Digests. Look up the topic and key number from Question 7 in each volume of the General Digest. Are there any cases from the United States Court of Appeals, Seventh Circuit digested under this topic and key number?

11b.   Perform Step 3 of updating the digest by looking at the "Closing with Cases Reported in" statement on the second page of the last General Digest on the shelf. According to the "Closing with Cases Reported in," what is the last volume of F.3d that this volume of the General Digest covers?

Now go to the *Federal Reporter 3d* and find the volume from Question 11b.

12b.   Each bound reporter volume has a small digest section in the back which gives you the topics and key numbers for the cases printed in that volume. Normally, you would check the digest sections of all of the bound reporters on the shelf beginning with the volume from Question 11b. For this assignment, however, check **only** the **most recent** bound volume. Are there any United States Court of Appeals, Seventh Circuit cases digested under your topic and key number?

13b. Now check the *Federal Reporter's* advance sheets. Bound volumes are updated by paperbound advance sheets. Several advance sheets are bound together into a reporter. In advance sheets, the digest section is in the front, just before the decisions begin. Normally, you would look at the digest section in all of the advance sheets for your topic and key number. For this assignment, however, check **only** the **most recent** advance sheet. Are there any United States Court of Appeals, Seventh Circuit cases digested under your topic and key number?

One great advantage of the West topic and key number system is that you can use it for **all jurisdictions**. The same topic and key number for a specific point of law can be used for researching all state and federal courts whose decisions are published in West reporters. Different West digests will group jurisdictions in different ways.

Regional digests contain state cases from each state covered by that particular region. The federal digests cover all of the federal courts, and the Decennial and General Digests, all of the state and federal jurisdictions. Use the most appropriate digest in your library, and provide the full citation, in correct form, for the following case. Search under the topic and key number from **Question 2**.

14. Check the *Texas Digest 2d* or the *Tenth Decennial Digest, Part 1*. Provide the citation in correct form of the 1988 Texas state Court of Appeals case digested under the topic and key number from Question 2. Omit any subsequent history in your citation.

ASSIGNMENT FOUR
FINDING CASES BY SUBJECT
EXERCISE C

GOALS OF THIS ASSIGNMENT:
To introduce you to finding cases by subject on Westlaw.
To give you practice at the various methods of using West's topics and key numbers.

CITATION RULES: For this assignment when citing a case, assume you are citing the case in a legal document that will be submitted to a state court that does not require parallel cites.

Please research federal cases for the Fourth Circuit. We need to know what evidence a plaintiff must prove in order to show she was discriminatorily denied equal pay and promotion because of her sex. Another attorney has given you a relevant case, *Soble v. University of Maryland*, a 1985 United States Court of Appeals, Fourth Circuit case which has a headnote on point. Use this case to find other relevant cases. This is called the "one good case" approach.

Sign on to Westlaw. Retrieve the case by party name.

Westlaw: Select **4th Circuit** as your jurisdiction. Use the **Title field search**: **TI(party & party)**.

1.   What is the West reporter cite for the case?

2.   Click on the link to the case. The relevant headnote for our issue is headnote two. What is the West topic and key number of headnote two?

3.   We now have a West topic and key number to begin our research for all Fourth Circuit cases with the same topic and key number. First, let's find out just what this topic and key number represent. Look at the topic and key number analysis for headnote two. What does the key number from Question 2 stand for? Include all relevant topics of which your key number may be a subtopic.

4.   Is there a 1999 United States Court of Appeals, Fourth Circuit case **arising out of Maryland** with at least one headnote digested under this topic and key number? If so, provide the full West reporter citation of the case according to Bluepages B10 and Rule 10 of *The Bluebook*.

     Westlaw: If the headnotes are not displayed, click on the West Headnotes header. If the key number classification hierarchy is not displayed next to your headnote, click on "Change View." When the view shows the classification hierarchy next to the headnote, click on the topic and key number link on the left in the last line to view the headnotes classified under the same topic and key number from your selected jurisdiction. You can apply a date filter to narrow your results.

5.   Now you will use the topic approach. The topic approach merely involves reading the list of key numbers and looking for a relevant topic that covers the point of law you are researching. If you were looking for civil rights cases concerning whether remedies under federal employment discrimination statutes are questions of law or fact, under what topic and key number would you look?

     Westlaw: Click on the Westlaw logo at the top of the page to go to the Westlaw home page. Click on the Tools tab in the Browse section of the home page, then click the West Key Number System link. You are looking at the alphabetical list of all West topics. Click on your topic to see the key numbers. The Roman numeral headings will help you find the relevant key number.

6.   Search for Fourth Circuit cases digested under your topic and key number from Question 5. What is the name of the 2006 United States Court of Appeals, Fourth Circuit case arising out of Maryland? **Tip:** You can narrow your results by using the jurisdiction and date filters on the left.

7.   Now you will use the keyword approach. With the keyword approach in Westlaw, you first select the jurisdiction in All Content that contains the cases from the jurisdiction you are researching. You are searching for United States Court of Appeals, Fourth Circuit civil rights cases dealing with whether Title VII provides the exclusive remedy for employment discrimination claims based on race against state employers or if a plaintiff can also bring a § 1983 action? Use the DIGEST (DI) field search to look for West topics, key numbers, and headnotes containing the keywords from your question. Examine the headnotes in the cases retrieved and look for the headnote covering the point of law for Civil Rights – Remedies under federal employment discrimination statutes – existence of other remedies, exclusivity. What topic and key number are assigned to this specific issue?

8.   What is the proper citation to the 1987 United States Court of Appeals, Fourth Circuit case arising out of Maryland that deals with the issue from Question 7 and has a headnote with the topic and key number from Question 7? **Tip:** You can narrow your results by using the jurisdiction and date filters on the left.

HOW CURRENT IS YOUR DIGEST RESEARCH ON WESTLAW?

When you conduct a topic and key number search on Westlaw, your results are as up to date as you would achieve doing your search in the West paper digest and completing all steps to update the digest in paper—digest volume, digest pocket part or pamphlet, digest interim pamphlet, hardbound reporter volumes, and reporter advance sheets.

One great advantage of the West topic and key number system is that you can use it for **all jurisdictions**. The same topic and key number for a specific point of law can be used for researching all state and federal courts whose decisions are published in West reporters.

When you already know the topic and key number you want to use in your search, you can bypass the Custom Digest page and run your search in one or several jurisdictions. First, you need to know the correct formula for creating your search.

Step 1. Determine the topic number for your topic. On Westlaw, the topic number can be seen before each topic assigned to the headnotes of the cases. The number can also be found in the West Key Number Digest Outline on Westlaw. Your search term will begin with this number.
Example: Topic: Adoption Topic number = 17

Step 2. Insert the letter "k" in your search to stand for "key number" next to your topic number. Do not insert a space between the topic number and the "k."

Step 3. Insert the key number you want to search next to the "k." Do not insert a space between the "k" and the key number.

Your search term formula is: "Topic number + k + Key number"
     Example: Adoption key number 5 (Persons who may adopt)
            Search term = **17k5**

9.   Use the formula above to create your search term for the topic and key number from **Question 2.** What is your search term?

      Select the appropriate jurisdiction to conduct a topic and key number digest search and provide the full citation, in correct form, for the following cases. Search using the topic and key number search term you created in **Question 9**.

10.   You want to determine if there are any Mississippi state cases that deal with what the court's findings as to sufficiency of evidence to support a jury's finding of a hostile work environment in a Title VII sexual harassment action. West editors would have assigned these cases the topic and key number from **Question 2**. Select Mississippi as your jurisdiction and conduct a search using the search term from **Question 9**. Provide the full regional citation, in correct form, of the 2012 Supreme Court of Mississippi case in your results. **Tip:** Use the date filter on the left.

11.   Assume you need to determine if there are any Tennessee cases dealing with this same topic. Select Tennessee as your jurisdiction and conduct a search using the search term from Question 9. What is the name of the 1999 Court of Appeals of Tennessee case that has a headnote with your topic and key number? **Tip:** Use the date filter on the left.

ASSIGNMENT FOUR
FINDING CASES BY SUBJECT
EXERCISE D

GOALS OF THIS ASSIGNMENT:
To introduce you to finding cases by subject on Lexis Advance.
To give you practice at the various methods of using LexisNexis topics.

CITATION RULES: For this assignment when citing a case, assume you are citing the case in a legal document that will be submitted to a state court that does not require parallel cites.

Please research federal cases for the Third Circuit. We want to find cases concerning costs and attorney fees under the Copyright Act, specifically whether fees are always mandated to the prevailing party. Another attorney has given you a relevant case, *Lieb v. Topstone Industries, Inc.*, a 1986 United States Court of Appeals, Third Circuit case which has a headnote on point. Use this case to find other relevant cases. This is called the "one good case" approach.
Sign on to **Lexis Advance**. Retrieve the case by party name.

Lexis Advance: Set the filters to **3rd Circuit** under Jurisdiction and Cases under Category. Conduct a **Name segment search** for the *Lieb v. Topstone Industries* decision. Find the case in the search results. **TIP:** When doing a **Name segment search** using party names replace the "v." with an ampersand. **Example: NAME(party & party).**

1.   What is the West reporter cite for the case?

2.   Scroll down and look at the LexisNexis headnotes. The relevant headnote for our issue is headnote four which has been assigned one topic. What is the topic for headnote four? Include all levels of the topic hierarchy as shown in the case.

3.   Notice that part of the topic has been left out. You can view the complete topic in the Topic Index. Click on the link for the fourth part of the topic that is your answer for Question 2, then click on "View in topic index." Use the back arrow at the bottom of the index to see each part of the topic. What is the complete topic from Question 2?

4.   Is there a 2003 United States Court of Appeals, Third Circuit case with at least one headnote assigned the same topic? If so, provide the full West reporter citation of the case according to Bluepages B10 and Rule 10 of *The Bluebook*.
Lexis Advance: Go back to our case. Click on the link for the fourth part of the topic for headnote four. Click on "Get documents." Use the filters on the left to narrow the results to the 3rd Circuit under Court and timeline of Jan 01, 2003 to Dec 31, 2003. Click OK.

5.   Now you will use the topic approach. The topic approach merely involves reading the list of topics and looking for a relevant topic that covers the point of law you are researching. If you were looking for cases concerning who is an indispensable party in a civil infringement action under copyright infringement actions, under what topic and subtopics would you look?
Lexis Advance: Click on **Browse** at the top of the page, then **Topics**. A list of topics is displayed alphabetically. Browse through the list of topics and navigate through the subtopics.

6.   What is the name of the 1958 United States Court of Appeals, Third Circuit with the topic from Question 5?
Lexis Advance: Click on that topic/subtopic from Question 5. Click on "Get documents." Use the filters on the left to narrow the results to the 3rd Circuit under Court and timeline of Jan 01, 1958 to Dec 31, 1958. Click OK.

7.   You can also search topics by keyword. Search for a topic that covers infringer's profits in civil infringement actions under copyright. Under what topics and subtopics would you look?
Lexis Advance: Click on **Browse** at the top of the page, then **Topics**. Type your keywords in the "Find a topic" search box.

8.   What is the proper citation of the 2011 United States Court of Appeals, Third Circuit case with a headnote containing the topic/subtopics from Question 7 that answers the question: to succeed on a copyright claim for **infringers' profits**, must a plaintiff first prove the defendants' gross revenues over the course of the relevant time period and then establish a causal nexus between the infringement and the profits sought? List the full West reporter citation of the case in correct form.

Lexis Advance: Click on that topic/subtopic from Question 7. Click on "Get documents." Use the filters on the left to narrow the results to the 3rd Circuit under Court and timeline of Jan 01, 2011 to Dec 31, 2011. Click OK.

HOW CURRENT IS YOUR DIGEST RESEARCH ON LEXIS ADVANCE?

When you conduct a topic search in a Lexis Advance source, your results are as current as the source file you are using. For example, most Lexis Advance sources are updated as soon as LexisNexis receives the case from the court that issued the opinion.

One advantage of the LexisNexis legal topic system is that you can use it for **all jurisdictions**. The same relevant topic/subtopic can be used for researching all state and federal courts whose decisions are included in the LexisNexis system.

Conduct a LexisNexis topic search and provide the full citation, in correct form, for the following cases. Search using the topic from **Question 3**. Narrow your search using the appropriate filters.

9.   State the name of the 2000 Commonwealth Court of Pennsylvania decision with a headnote with the topic from Question 3.

Lexis Advance: Click on **Browse** at the top of the page, then **Topics**. Browse through the list of topics and navigate through the subtopics to the topic/subtopic from Question 3. Click on "Get documents." Use the filters on the left to narrow the results to the Pennsylvania under Court – State and timeline of Jan 01, 2000 to Dec 31, 2000. Click OK.

10.   Are there any United States Court of Appeals, Fifth Circuit cases with this same topic. What is the name of the 2008 Fifth Circuit decision?

Lexis Advance: Clear your previous filters. Apply new filters for 5th Circuit under Court and timeline of Jan 01, 2008 to Dec 31, 2008. Click OK.

ASSIGNMENT FIVE
UPDATING AND VALIDATING CASES–CITATORS
EXERCISE A

GOAL OF THIS ASSIGNMENT:
To teach you how to identify case history and case treatment in a Shepard's entry in paper.

> You are researching federal law from the Fifth Circuit for a brief you are writing. The subject of the brief concerns double jeopardy and what constitutes same offenses under double jeopardy. You have found a case that you would like to use in your brief but first need to update the case to verify it is still good law and also want to use the case to expand your research.

CITATION RULES: When a case cite appears in your answers, use the standard abbreviation for the reporter as found in *The Bluebook: A Uniform System of Citation*, 20th ed. It may differ substantially from the Shepard's abbreviation. Do not include the case name in your answers.

> **For questions 1-4, Shepardize *United States v. Lankford*, 196 F.3d 563 (5th Cir. 1999). Find the case in the <u>bound</u> *Shepard's Federal Citations* volume that contains cites to it.**

1. To verify whether or not a case is good law, you must look at the direct history of the case and the negative indirect history. Shepardize the case. Did the United States Supreme Court deny certiorari to your case? **TIP:** Look after the year of your case. Is there an entry that reads **US cert den**?

2. Has a United States Court of Appeals, Fifth Circuit case cited the *Lankford* case for *Lankford's* headnote 23? **Hint**: Look for a superscript 23 after the reporter abbreviation (F3d). If so, state the cite as listed in Shepard's. Remember, Shepard's in print does not list the first page of the case, but only the actual page that cites your case.

3. What is the cite of the **first listed** court of appeals decision under the Fifth Circuit that followed the *Lankford* case?

4.   Has an A.L.R. Fed. annotation cited *Lankford*? If so, state the cite to the annotation.

        Reshelve Shepard's Citations.

5.   Look up the case in your answer to Question 2. Does this case deal with double jeopardy as one of its issues?

        The attorney for whom you are clerking has asked you to help on another research assignment. She is researching termination of government employees. She has found a United States Supreme Court decision *Service v. Dulles* that indicates that the government must abide by regulations in place when terminating an employee. She has asked you to update this case.

        Shepardize U.S. Supreme Court case *Service v. Dulles*, 354 U.S. 363, 77 S. Ct. 1152, 1 L. Ed. 2d 1403. Examine the spine of *Shepard's United States Citations–United States Reports*, Volumes 1.1-1.11 and find the volume in which your case appears to answer Questions 6-12.

6.   How does Shepard's show parallel cites?

7.   What is the cite of the same case in the federal court of appeals?

8.   What is the cite of the United States Supreme Court decision that distinguished the *Service* case?

9.   What is the West reporter cite of the Delaware decision that cited the *Service* case? If more than one case is listed, give the cite for the **first listed** case.

10.   What First Circuit court of appeals case's dissent cited *Service*?

11.   State the Shepard's entry for the **first** listed A.L.R. Fed. annotation that cited *Service*.

12.   Did the A.L.R. reference in the previous question appear in the annotation or its supplement? If you need help with this question, refer to the preface.

ASSIGNMENT FIVE
UPDATING AND VALIDATING CASES–CITATORS
EXERCISE B

GOAL OF THIS ASSIGNMENT:
To teach you how to identify case history and case treatment in a Shepard's entry in paper.

You are researching federal law from the Seventh Circuit for a brief you are writing. The subject of the brief concerns federal criminal conspiracy law. You have found a case that you would like to use in your brief but first need to update the case to verify it is still good law and also want to use the case to expand your research.

CITATION RULES: When a case cite appears in your answers, use the standard abbreviation for the reporter as found in *The Bluebook: A Uniform System of Citation*, 20th ed. It may differ substantially from the Shepard's abbreviation. Do not include the case name in your answers.

For questions 1-4, Shepardize *United States v. Paiz*, 905 F.2d 1014 (7th Cir. 1990). Find the case in the **bound** *Shepard's Federal Citations* volume that contains cites to it.

1.   To verify whether or not a case is good law, you must look at the direct history of the case and the negative indirect history. Shepardize the case. Did the United States Supreme Court deny certiorari to your case? **TIP:** Look after the year of your case. Is there an entry that read **US cert den**?

2.   Have any United States Court of Appeals, Seventh Circuit cases cited the *Paiz* case for *Paiz's* headnote 2? **Hint**: Look for a superscript 2 after the reporter abbreviation (F2d or F3d). If so, state the **first listed** cite as listed in Shepard's. Remember, Shepard's in print does not list the first page of the case, but only the actual page that cites your case.

3.   What is the cite of the United States Court of Appeals decision from the Seventh Circuit that explained the *Paiz* case?

4.   Has an A.L.R. Fed. annotation cited *Paiz*? If so, state the cite.

          Reshelve Shepard's Citations.

5.   Look up the case in your answer to Question 2. Does this case deal with conspiracy as one of its issues?

          The attorney for whom you are clerking has asked you to help on another research assignment. She is researching whether a town ordinance can prohibit "For Sale" and "Sold" signs on residential property. She has found a United States Supreme Court decision *Linmark Associates, Inc. v. Township of Willingboro* that indicates that such a ban violates the First Amendment. She has asked you to update this case.

          Shepardize the U.S. Supreme Court case *Linmark Associates, Inc. v. Township of Willingboro*, 431 U.S. 85, 97 S. Ct. 1614, 52 L. Ed. 2d 155. Examine the spine of *Shepard's United States Citations–United States Reports*, Volumes 1.1-1.11 and find the volume in which your case appears to answer Questions 6-12.

6.   How does Shepard's show parallel cites?

7.   What is the cite of the same case in the federal court of appeals?

8.   What is the cite of the United States Supreme Court decision that distinguished the *Linmark* case?

9.   What is the West reporter cite of the Maine decision that cited the *Linmark* case? If more than one case is listed, give the cite for the **first listed** case.

10.   What Seventh Circuit court of appeals case's dissent cited *Linmark*?

11.   State the Shepard's entry for the A.L.R. Fed. annotation that cited *Linmark*.

12.   Did the A.L.R. reference in the previous question appear in the annotation or its supplement? If you need help with this question, refer to the preface.

1. Describe the steps ... one of the above session into a physical bundle ...

2. What is an Oracle fault...

3. ...

4. ...

ASSIGNMENT FIVE
UPDATING AND VALIDATING CASES–CITATORS
EXERCISE C

GOAL OF THIS ASSIGNMENT:
To teach you how to identify case history and case treatment in Westlaw's KeyCite.

You are researching federal civil rights law from the Fourth Circuit for a brief you are writing. The subject of the brief deals with employment discrimination under federal statutes. You have found a case that you would like to use in your brief but first need to update the case to verify it is still good law and also want to use the case to expand your research.

CITATION RULES: When a case cite appears in your answers, use the standard abbreviation for the reporter as found in *The Bluebook: A Uniform System of Citation*, 20th ed. It may differ substantially from the Shepard's abbreviation. Do not include the case name in your answers, unless specifically told to provide the name.

For questions 1-5, KeyCite *Soble v. University of Maryland*, 778 F.2d 164 (4th Cir. 1985). Log on to Westlaw.

1. To verify whether or not a case is good law, you must look at the direct history of the case and the negative indirect history. KeyCite the case. Look at the **History** tab. Does our case have any direct history? In other words, was our case appealed?

2. If there are any citing cases that negatively impact your case they will be listed under the **Negative Treatment** tab. Are there any such cases? If so, what is the name of the 2001 case that distinguished *Soble*?

    To see all cases and documents that cite *Soble*, click on the Citing References tab.

3. You can limit your display of cases citing *Soble* to cases that cite *Soble* for points of law in *Soble's* West headnotes. What is the cite of the 2004 case that cited *Soble* for the point of law in West headnote 2?
    Westlaw: Under **View**, click **Cases**. Under Headnote Topics, click **specify** for Civil Rights. Select headnote 2 (Civil Rights K. 1549). Click **Apply Filters**.

4.   Link to the case from Question 3. Read the case. Does this case deal with employment discrimination under federal statutes?

5.   If you were to cite the case that you linked to in Question 4 in your brief, would the case be mandatory or persuasive authority in the Fourth Circuit?

       Go back to KeyCite. Click on Undo Filters in Westlaw before completing the next question.

6.   You are looking for an A.L.R. Fed. annotation that cites *Soble*. What is the cite of the A.L.R. Fed. annotation originally published in 1971 that cites *Soble*? **Tip:** Narrow your view to ALR under Secondary Sources.

       The attorney for whom you are clerking has asked you to help on another research assignment dealing with antitrust law. She has found a United States Supreme Court decision *Brown Shoe Co. v. United States* that considered whether the merger of two companies substantially lessened competition or created a monopoly in violation of the Clayton Act. She has asked you to update this case.

       KeyCite the U.S. Supreme Court case *Brown Shoe Co. v. United States*, 370 U.S. 294, 82 S. Ct. 1502, 8 L. Ed. 2d 510.

7.   What KeyCite signal has been assigned to the *Brown Shoe* case?

8.   Look at the **Negative Treatment** tab. What is the cite of the 1999 Eastern District of Texas decision that indicates *Brown Shoe* was superseded by statute?

       To see all cases and documents that cite *Brown Shoe*, click on the Citing References tab.

9. What is the West reporter cite of the positive United States Supreme Court case decided on Mar. 19, 1974 that examined the *Brown Shoe* case?
   Westlaw: To narrow the results, follow these steps: Under **View**, click **Cases**. Under **Jurisdiction**, expand **Federal** and select **Supreme Court**. Under **Depth of Treatment**, click the four green bars. Click **Apply Filters** and find the case in the results.

   Click Undo Filters before completing the next question.

10. What is the West reporter cite of the 1992 Colorado state decision that cited the *Brown Shoe* case?
    Westlaw: To narrow the results, follow these steps: Under **View**, make sure you have selected **Cases**. Under **Jurisdiction**, expand **State** and select **Colorado**. Click on **Apply Filters** and find your case.

    Click Undo Filters before completing the next question.

11. What is the name of the United States Supreme Court decision decided on June 8, 1992 whose dissent cited *Brown Shoe*?
    Westlaw: To narrow the results, follow these steps: Under **View**, make sure you have selected **Cases**. Under **Narrow**, type **dissent** in the **Search within results** box and click **Continue**. Under **Jurisdiction**, expand **Federal** and select **Supreme Court**. Click **Apply Filters** and examine the cases in the results to obtain your answer.

    Westlaw's Table of Authorities feature allows you to retrieve a list of cases cited in your case.

12. Click on the **Table of Authorities** tab at the top of the case. How many cases were cited in *Brown Shoe*?

ASSIGNMENT FIVE
UPDATING AND VALIDATING CASES–CITATORS
EXERCISE D

GOAL OF THIS ASSIGNMENT:
To teach you how to identify case history and case treatment in Shepard's on Lexis Advance.

You are researching federal law from the Third Circuit for a brief you are writing. The subject of the brief deals with costs and attorney fees available under the Copyright Act. You have found a case that you would like to use in your brief but first need to update the case to verify it is still good law and also want to use the case to expand your research.

CITATION RULES: When a case cite appears in your answers, use the standard abbreviation for the reporter as found in *The Bluebook: A Uniform System of Citation*, 20th ed. It may differ substantially from the Shepard's abbreviation. Do not include the case name in your answers, unless specifically told to provide the name.

For questions 1-5, Shepardize *Lieb v. Topstone Industries, Inc.*, 788 F.2d 151 (3d Cir. 1986). Log on to Lexis Advance.

1.   To verify whether or not a case is good law, you must look at the direct history of the case and negative indirect history. Shepardize the case. Use Shepard's in **List** view. Is there any **Subsequent Appellate History** for this case?
Lexis Advance: Navigate to the **Appellate History** report section and look at the report section at the top.

2.   Look at the negative indirect history cases for *Lieb*. What is the name of the 1986 United States Court of Appeals, Third Circuit decision that distinguishes *Lieb*?
Lexis Advance: Navigate to the **Citing Decisions** report section. Under **Narrow By**, look at the **Analysis** section. Click on the **Distinguished by** under **Caution**.

Click Clear before completing the next question.

3. Remember that the Lexis Advance online version of the *Lieb* opinion has been assigned LexisNexis topics and headnotes. What is the cite of the 2000 United States Court of Appeals, Third Circuit decision that cited *Lieb* for the point of law in LexisNexis headnote 3?
    Lexis Advance: Under **Narrow By**, click on **3rd Circuit** under **Court** and **HN3** under **Headnotes**.

4. Link to the case from Question 3. Does this case discuss awarding attorney fees?

5. If you were to cite the case that you linked to in Question 4 in your brief, would the case be mandatory or persuasive authority in the Third Circuit?

Click Clear before completing the next question.

6. You are looking for a law review article that cites *Lieb*. What is the cite of the 2011 Drake Law Review article that cites *Lieb*?
    Lexis Advance: Navigate to the **Other Citing Sources** report section. Under **Narrow By**, click on **Law Reviews** under **Content**. Look through your results.

The attorney for whom you are clerking has asked you to help on another research assignment. She is researching whether an individual's grand jury testimony may be used as evidence of perjury if she was not told of her Fifth Amendment right to remain silent prior to testifying. She has found a United States Supreme Court decision *United States v. Wong* that is relevant. She has asked you to update this case.

Shepardize U.S. Supreme Court case *United States v. Wong*, 431 U.S. 174, 97 S. Ct. 1823, 52 L. Ed. 2d 231.

7.   What Shepard's signal has been assigned to the *Wong* case?

8.   Look at the **Prior History** section. What is the West reporter cite to the *Wong* case from the United States Court of Appeals, Ninth Circuit?

9.   What is the cite for the 1989 Northern District of West Virginia decision that distinguished *Wong*?
        Lexis Advance: Navigate to the **Citing Decisions** report section. Under **Narrow By**, look at the **Analysis** section. Click on the **Distinguished by** under **Caution**. Scroll down to review the cases.

        Click Clear before completing the next question.

10.   What is the West reporter cite of the 1982 Pennsylvania Superior Court decision that cited the *Wong* case?
        Lexis Advance: Under **Narrow by**, look at the **Court** section. Click on **Pennsylvania** under **State Courts**.

        Click Clear before completing the next question.

11.   What is the West reporter cite of the 2004 United States Court of Appeals, Fourth Circuit case whose dissent cited *Wong*? Give the cite to the dissenting opinion.
        Lexis Advance: Under **Narrow By**, look at the **Court** section. Click on **4th Circuit** under **Federal Courts**.

        Lexis Advance's Table of Authorities feature allows you to retrieve a list of all of the cases cited in your case.

12.   Retrieve the Table of Authorities for the *Wong* case. How many cases were cited in *Wong*?
        Lexis Advance: Click to navigate to the **Table of Authorities** report section.

ASSIGNMENT SIX
AMERICAN LAW REPORTS
EXERCISE A

GOALS OF THIS ASSIGNMENT:
To give you practice at using the A.L.R. tables and indexes.
To find whether a relevant annotation has been superseded or supplemented.

>   You are researching double jeopardy. You are interested in how an acquittal
>   or conviction in state court affects the ability to prosecute the same act or
>   transaction in federal court. Use the Index to A.L.R. to find a relevant A.L.R.
>   Fed. annotation by subject.

1.   What is the cite to the A.L.R. Fed. annotation?

Find the annotation from 18 A.L.R. Fed. and answer Questions 2-10.

2.   What is the correct citation of the annotation itself? (See Rule 16.7.6 of *The Bluebook*.)

3.   Remember, the full text of an opinion accompanies each annotation that explains
      the law in the case's subject area. This case is referenced at the bottom of the first
      page of the annotation or published right before the annotation in earlier volumes.
      State the full West reporter citation of the opinion whose text is printed in full.
      Use proper *Bluebook* form.

4. Go back to the annotation. To which section of the Am. Jur. 2d topic *Criminal Law* could you turn to find related material?

5. Examine the Index section. Which section discusses double jeopardy?

6. Examine the Table of Courts and Circuits. This table will quickly tell you all jurisdictions covered by the annotation. Are any Fifth Circuit cases discussed in this annotation?

7. Examine the scope and the references to related matters in the Introduction section. State the cite of the annotation listed which discusses the modern status of the doctrine of res judicata in criminal cases.

8. Examine § 4[a]. What 1971 Fifth Circuit Court of Appeals decision is cited in this section? State its name.

9. Look at the beginning of the annotation in the pocket part to this volume. Examine the beginning of the updating material for a note telling you that the annotation has been superseded. Is there a note telling you that this annotation has been superseded?

10. The pocket parts in A.L.R.3d, 4th, 5th, 6th, Fed., and Fed. 2d volumes provide updated text, recent cases, and additional related annotations. Provide the cite to the annotation on double jeopardy considerations in federal criminal cases—Supreme Court cases.

    Reshelve the A.L.R. and find the volume *A.L.R. Table of Laws, Rules, and Regulations*.

11. You can also tell if an annotation has been superseded by looking in the Annotation History Table, found in the *A.L.R. Table of Laws, Rules, and Regulations* volume and its pocket part. Has 7 A.L.R. Fed. 855 been superseded? If so, state the cite of the superseding annotation.

ASSIGNMENT SIX
AMERICAN LAW REPORTS
EXERCISE B

GOALS OF THIS ASSIGNMENT:
To give you practice at using the A.L.R. tables and indexes.
To find whether a relevant annotation has been superseded or supplemented.

You are researching federal law to determine whether a defendant's similar prior acts are admissible in a federal conspiracy prosecution. Use the Index to A.L.R. to find a relevant A.L.R. Fed. annotation by subject.

1.   What is the cite to the A.L.R. Fed. annotation?

Find the annotation from 20 A.L.R. Fed. and answer Questions 2-10.

2.   What is the correct citation of the annotation itself? (See Rule 16.7.6 of *The Bluebook*.)

3.   Remember, the full text of an opinion accompanies each annotation that explains the law in the case's subject area. This case is referenced at the bottom of the first page of the annotation or published right before the annotation in earlier volumes. State the full West reporter citation of the opinion whose text is printed in full. Use proper *Bluebook* form.

4.   Go back to the annotation. To which section of the Am. Jur. 2d topic *Conspiracy* could you turn to find related material?

5. Examine the Index section. Which section discusses passing counterfeit obligations?

6. Examine the Table of Courts and Circuits. This table will quickly tell you all jurisdictions covered by the annotation. Are any Seventh Circuit cases discussed in this annotation?

7. Examine the scope and the references to related matters in the Introduction section. State the cite of the annotation listed which deals with the admissibility of evidence as to other offense as affected by defendant's acquittal of that offense.

8. Examine § 4[c]. What 1913 United States Supreme Court decision is cited in this section? State its name.

9. Look up the cite to the annotation in the pocket part to this volume. Examine the beginning of the updating material for a note telling you that the annotation has been superseded. Is there a note telling you that this annotation has been superseded?

10. The pocket parts in A.L.R.3d, 4th, 5th, 6th, Fed., and Fed. 2d volumes also provide information on later cases that are relevant to the annotation. Provide the name of the United States Court of Appeals, Third Circuit that updates § 3 of the annotation and indicates that evidence of another offense is not admissible.

    Reshelve the A.L.R. and find the volume *A.L.R. Table of Laws, Rules, and Regulations*.

11. You can also tell if an annotation has been superseded by looking in the Annotation History Table, found in the *A.L.R. Table of Laws, Rules, and Regulations* volume and its pocket part. Has 12 A.L.R. Fed. 910 been superseded? If so, state the cite of the superseding annotation.

ASSIGNMENT SIX
AMERICAN LAW REPORTS
EXERCISE C

GOALS OF THIS ASSIGNMENT:
To give you practice finding an A.L.R. on Westlaw.
To find whether a relevant annotation has been superseded or supplemented.

You are researching federal law to determine whether wage differentials violate the provisions of Title VII of the Civil Rights Act of 1964 which prohibit sex discrimination in employment. Find an *American Law Reports* annotation on this topic.

Sign on to Westlaw. Select American Law Reports as your content.

Westlaw: In the **All Content** tab under **Browse**, click on **Secondary Sources.** Look under **By Type** and click on **American Law Reports.** Type your search terms in the search bar.

1.   What is the cite to the A.L.R. Fed. annotation?

Click on the link to the 62 A.L.R. Fed. and answer Questions 2-10.

2.   What is the correct citation of the annotation itself **in print**? (See Rule 16.7.6 of *The Bluebook.*) **Note**: Westlaw provides the copyright date of the print volume in the "originally published" parenthetical.

3.   Read the text of section 3 of the annotation. This annotation was inspired by a federal decision dealing with the same subject matter. The opinion can be found in a West reporter and in the same volume as your annotation. State the full West reporter citation of the 1980 Third Circuit opinion whose text is printed in full in the same print A.L.R. volume.

4.   Go to the **Research References** section that is found at the end of the annotation. Scroll down to the Legal Encyclopedia section. To which sections of the Am. Jur. 2d topic *Civil Rights* could you turn to find related material?

5.   Go to the Index section. Examine the Index section. Which section discusses the occupation of library assistant?

6.   Examine the Table of Cases, Laws, and Rules. This table will quickly tell you all jurisdictions covered by the annotation. Are any Fourth Circuit cases discussed in this annotation?

7.   Go back down to the **Research References** and scroll to the A.L.R. Library section that lists related annotations. State the cite of the annotation listed whose subject is the construction and application of Lilly Ledbetter Fair Pay Act of 2009.

8.   Examine § 5[a]. A 1977 United States Court of Appeals, Fourth Circuit decision is cited in this section. State its name.

9.   In this online version of the annotation, information from the pocket part or cumulative supplement is added at the end of each section. This information includes later cases that are relevant to the annotation. Look at the Cumulative Supplement for § 5[a]. Provide the name of the 1984 United States District Court, Middle District of North Carolina decision that updates § 5[a] of the annotation.

10.   Look at the beginning of your A.L.R. annotation. According to the note, how frequently are the A.L.R. databases updated with relevant new cases?

11.   The ALR database on Westlaw contains electronic annotations (e-annos). These annotations are not available in print and are identified by a citation that uses the year for the volume number and the number of the annotation for that year as the page number. **Example: 2007 A.L.R.6th 1.** Retrieve 2011 A.L.R. Fed. 2d 1 by citation. What is the title of this annotation?

12.   You can also tell if an annotation has been superseded by looking for a KeyCite red flag or by a note indicating the annotation has been superceded. Has the electronic annotation from Question 11 (2011 A.L.R. Fed. 2d 1) been superseded? If so, state the cite of the superseding annotation.

ASSIGNMENT SIX
AMERICAN LAW REPORTS
EXERCISE D

GOALS OF THIS ASSIGNMENT:
To give you practice finding an A.L.R. on Lexis Advance.
To find whether a relevant annotation has been superseded or supplemented.

You are researching federal law to determine under what conditions there is a right to an award of attorney fees under the Copyright Act, 17 U.S.C.A. § 505. Find an *American Law Reports* annotation on this topic.

Sign on to Lexis Advance and select the American Law Reports source.

Lexis Advance: On the **Content Type** tab, click on **Secondary Materials.** Under Federal, click on the **American Law Reports (ALR)** link. In the red search box, enter the keywords for your search.

1. What is the cite to the A.L.R. Fed. annotation? **Note:** Scan your results for the annotation dealing with the Copyright Act, 17 U.S.C.A. § 505.

Click on the link to the 174 A.L.R. Fed. and answer Questions 2-10.

2. What is the correct citation of the annotation itself **in print**? (See Rule 16.7.6 of *The Bluebook*.) **Note**: The date of the annotation is **2001**—this information cannot be discerned on Lexis Advance.

3. This annotation was inspired by a federal decision dealing with the same subject matter. Read the text of section 7[a] of the annotation which mentions the inspiring federal decision. The opinion can be found in a West reporter and in the same volume as your annotation. State the full West reporter citation of the 2000 Southern District of West Virginia opinion whose text is printed in full in the same print A.L.R. volume.

4.   Go to the **Table of References** section that is found at the end of the annotation. Scroll down to the Legal Encyclopedia section. To which sections of the Am. Jur. 2d topic *Copyright and Literary Property* could you turn to find related material?

5.   Go to the **Index of Terms** section. Examine the Index section. Which section discusses bad faith in litigation?

6.   Examine the **Jurisdictional Table of Statutes and Cases**. This table will quickly tell you all jurisdictions covered by the annotation. Are any Second Circuit cases discussed in this annotation?

7.   At the beginning of the annotation, go to section **[1b] Related annotations** under section **[1] Introduction**. Here, you will find related annotations listed. State the cite of the annotation listed whose subject is judicial decisions involving ASCAP.

8.   Examine section **[3a]**. A 1993 United States Court of Appeals, First Circuit decision is cited in this section. State its name.

9.   In this online version of the annotation, information from the pocket part or cumulative supplement is added at the end of each section. This information includes later cases that are relevant to the annotation. Look at the Cumulative Cases for section **[3a]**. Provide the name of the 2007 First Circuit case that updates section **[3a]** of the annotation.

10.   Look at the beginning of your A.L.R. annotation. According to the note, how frequently are the A.L.R. databases updated with relevant new cases?

11.   Lexis Advance will also indicate if the annotation you try to read has been superseded by another annotation. Retrieve by citation 12 A.L.R. Fed. 951. Has this annotation been superseded?
        Lexis Advance: If American Law Reports (ALR) is not currently set as your search filter, set it by using the following steps: Click on **Browse** at the top of the page, then click on **Sources**. In the **Find a Source** search box, type **American Law Reports** and click **Search**. Click on **American Law Reports (ALR)** in the list. Click **Add source as a search filter**. In the red search box, type **CITE(12 a.l.r. fed. 951)**.

12.   What is the cite of the annotation that superseded the annotation you searched for in Question 11?

ASSIGNMENT SEVEN
REVIEW—FINDING, CITING, AND UPDATING CASES
EXERCISE A

GOALS OF THIS ASSIGNMENT:
To review the use of digests, citators in print or online, and A.L.R. to find cases.
To combine several steps of a research strategy using different types of materials.

You are working for defense attorney Mitch Grisham's firm in Memphis, Tennessee. Bill Harrison is a client of the firm. Grisham wants to file a motion to suppress evidence that was discovered in Bill Harrison's house when police executed a search warrant. Harrison contends that the affidavit in support of the warrant contained intentionally false statements and did not support probable cause. Attorney Grisham has asked you to research the law and cases that deal with **search and seizure** and the use of a **confidential informer** whose identity is known to the police to establish **probable cause** for a **federal search warrant** where the informer has provided **reliable information in the past**. Please research federal case law to determine how the court may deal with this situation. Before you begin, identify the federal jurisdiction that includes Tennessee and determine which courts' cases will be mandatory authority in that jurisdiction.

1.   If you are unfamiliar with a topic and looking for citations to primary authority for your jurisdiction, a good place to begin your research is in the A.L.R. Go to the A.L.R. Index and look for an A.L.R. Fed. annotation that may help you research this issue. What is the cite to the annotation?

Find the 196 A.L.R. Fed. annotation.

2.   What is the correct citation of the annotation itself? (See Rule 16.7.6 of *The Bluebook*.)

3.   In section 20[b], this annotation cites to a 1990 United States Court of Appeals, Sixth Circuit decision where the court found probable cause for the issuance of the warrant did not exist even though the informant had recently observed the crime or evidence of the crime. Provide the full West reporter citation to the case in correct format.

Find the case from Question 3 and read it.

4.   Given your fact situation, is this case on point?

5.   Is a United States Court of Appeals, Sixth Circuit case that is still good law mandatory or persuasive authority if cited to a federal district court in Tennessee?

6.   Look at the headnotes of this case. Several headnotes are relevant to your issue. Which headnote indicates that a defendant who challenges the veracity of statements in an affidavit in support of a search warrant must prove by a preponderance of the evidence that the false statements were made either intentionally or with reckless disregard for the truth? List its number, e.g., first, second, third, etc.

7.   What is the topic and key number of this headnote?

8.   Read the opinion corresponding to the point of law for the above headnote. If the challenged statement is removed from an affidavit and probable cause exists based on the affidavit absent the challenged statement, is the defendant entitled to a further hearing on the matter?

9.   Use *West's Federal Practice Digest 4th* to find other cases that are mandatory authority in your jurisdiction and have been assigned the same relevant topic and key number from Question 7. Provide the full citation in the West reporter for the 2008 decision. **Tip:** Hardbound volumes are updated with pocket parts or soft bound supplements.

You have decided to use the Sixth Circuit case from Question 3 in the memo that you are writing. You must verify that the case is still good law. You can also expand your research to other relevant cases through Shepard's. Shepardize the case in the bound main volume.

10.   Look at the front of the Shepard's at the "Case Analysis--Abbreviations" at the front of the volume. Study the abbreviations for the "History of Cases." Now find the listing for the cite of your case in the volume. Is there any direct history for your case indicating it was appealed to the United States Supreme Court?

11.   Turn back to the abbreviations at the front of the volume. Look at the abbreviations under "Treatment of Cases." Note that your case has been cited in several other Sixth Circuit cases. As you proceed in your research, you will need to look at these cases to determine if these cases are relevant to your issue. Have any of the Sixth Circuit decisions distinguished the *Bennett* case?

12.   Examine the case listings under the Sixth Circuit. Have any of the cases cited *Bennett* for the point of law discussed in the second headnote? If so, provide the cite of the entry.

Look up the case from Question 12.

13.   What is the name of the case in proper *Bluebook* format?

14.   Does the case discuss the issue of statements in a search warrant affidavit that are intentionally false or made with reckless disregard for the truth?

ASSIGNMENT SEVEN
REVIEW—FINDING, CITING, AND UPDATING CASES
EXERCISE B

GOALS OF THIS ASSIGNMENT:
To review the use of digests, citators in print or online, and A.L.R. to find cases.
To combine several steps of a research strategy using different types of materials.

Last week, the Abernathy law firm in Los Angeles, California was retained by Marcia Grant. Ms. Grant claims her employer is violating the Age Discrimination in Employment Act (ADEA). The employer recently implemented a neutrally imposed salary restructuring plan that disproportionately affected workers over the age of 40 and was not justified by business necessity. Ms. Grant claims that this policy has a disparate impact on employees at her work who are over the age of 40. You know that the ADEA protects employees from negative disparate treatment based on age. You have been asked to research whether the ADEA recognizes claims of **age discrimination** based on the **disparate impact** an employer's neutral policy may have on its employees. Please research federal case law to determine how the court may deal with this situation. Before you begin, identify the federal jurisdiction that includes California and determine which courts' cases will be mandatory authority in that jurisdiction.

1.   If you are unfamiliar with a topic and looking for citations to primary authority for your jurisdiction, a good place to begin your research is in the A.L.R. Go to the A.L.R. Index and look for an A.L.R. Fed. annotation that may help you research this issue. What is the cite to the annotation?

Find the 186 A.L.R. Fed. annotation.

2.   What is the correct citation of the annotation itself? (See Rule 16.7.6 of *The Bluebook*.)

3.   In section 6[b], this annotation cites to a 2000 United States Court of Appeals, Ninth Circuit decision. Provide the full West reporter citation to the case in correct format.

       Find the case from Question 3 and read it.

4.   Given your fact situation, is this case on point?

5.   Is a United States Court of Appeals, Ninth Circuit case that is still good law mandatory or persuasive authority if cited to a federal district court in California?

6.   Look at the headnotes of this case. Several headnotes are relevant to your issue. Which headnote states the disparate impact claims are cognizable under the ADEA? List its number, e.g., first, second, third, etc.

7.   What is the topic and key number of this headnote?

8.   Read the opinion corresponding to the point of law for the above headnote. What are the four listed things that the ADEA prohibits employers from discriminating against based on the individual's age?

9.   Use *West's Federal Practice Digest 4th* to find other cases that are mandatory authority in your jurisdiction and have been assigned the same relevant topic and key number from Question 7. However, West has reclassified this key number under the same topic **Civil Rights** but to new key number **1211**. Use the topic **Civil Rights** and **new** key number **1211** to find the 2008 Supreme Court of the United States decision digested under the **new** topic and key number whose annotation discusses disparate impact claims under ADEA. Provide the full citation in the official reports for the 2008 decision.

You have decided to use the Ninth Circuit case from Question 3 in the memo that you are writing. You must verify that the case is still good law. You can also expand your research to other relevant cases through Shepard's. Shepardize the case in the bound main volumes.

10.   Look at the front of the Shepard's at the "Case Analysis--Abbreviations" at the front of the volume. Study the abbreviations for the "History of Cases." Now find the listing for the cite of your case in the volume. Is there any direct history for your case indicating it was appealed to the United States Supreme Court?

11.   Turn back to the abbreviations at the front of the volume. Look at the abbreviations under "Treatment of Cases." Note that your case has been cited in several other Ninth Circuit cases. As you proceed in your research, you will need to look at these cases to determine if these cases are relevant to your issue. State the cite of the Ninth Circuit Court of Appeals case that distinguished your case.

12.   Examine the case listings under the Ninth Circuit. Have any of the cases cited *Katz* for the point of law discussed in the seventh headnote? If so, provide the cite that cites *Katz* for its seventh headnote.

Look up the case from Question 12.

13.   What is the name of the case in proper *Bluebook* format?

14.   Does this case deal with a disparate impact age discrimination claim under the ADEA?

ASSIGNMENT SEVEN
REVIEW—FINDING, CITING, AND UPDATING CASES
EXERCISE C

GOALS OF THIS ASSIGNMENT:
To review the use of Westlaw to find cases using headnotes, KeyCite, and A.L.R.
To combine several steps of a research strategy using different types of materials.

You are working as a summer associate for the Corbett Law Firm in New York City. Attorney Eddie Bixby has asked you to conduct research for one of his cases involving client Brandon Tinker, an architect. Mr. Tinker claims that MKJ architectural firm is misrepresenting that the Tinker's architectural drawings for a new building at a local university were produced by MKJ. You know the Lanham Act prohibits the use of false designation of origin of goods or services which would likely cause confusion as to the origin of the goods or services. Your assignment is to research the doctrine of **"reverse passing off"** under the **Lanham Act**. Please research federal case law to determine how the court may treat such a case. Before you begin, identify the federal jurisdiction that includes New York and determine which courts' cases will be mandatory authority in that jurisdiction.

Sign on to Westlaw. If you need help navigating through Westlaw, please go back to the prior assignments to see specific instructions.

1. If you are unfamiliar with a topic and looking for citations to primary authority for your jurisdiction, a good place to begin your research is in the American Law Reports. Search for an applicable A.L.R. Fed. annotation. What is the cite to the A.L.R. Fed. annotation?

Click on the 194 A.L.R. Fed. annotation.

2. What is the correct citation of the annotation itself? (See Rule 16.7.6 of *The Bluebook*.)

3.   Read section 2[b]. What is the 1999 United States Court of Appeals, Second Circuit case cited in footnote 3? Provide the full West reporter citation in correct format.

Click on the link for the case from Question 3 and read it.

4.   Given your fact situation, is this case on point?

5.   Is a United States Court of Appeals, Second Circuit case that is still good law mandatory or persuasive authority if cited to a federal district court in New York?

6.   Look at the headnotes of this case. Several headnotes are relevant to your issue. Which headnote states that the plaintiff could not establish a claim of reverse passing off under the Lanham Act against architects who allegedly falsely represented that they were the creators of plaintiff's copyrighted design drawings for hospital modernization project since the plaintiff could not show substantial similarity in the drawings? List its number, e.g., first, second, third, etc.

7.   What is the topic and key number of this headnote?

8.   Click on the headnote number to jump to the opinion section corresponding to the point of law for the above headnote. Read the section. What is the name of the 1994 case that supports plaintiff's observation that section 43(a) of the Lanham Act has been construed to prohibit misrepresenting the source of a product?

9.   Go up to the headnote from Question 6. Provide the full West reporter citation to the 1995 United States Court of Appeals, Second Circuit case digested under the same topic and key number.

KeyCite the case from Question 3.

10.   Look at the Direct History for your case. Is there any prior or subsequent history listed?

11.   What is the West reporter cite of the 2012 United States Court of Appeals, Second Circuit case that distinguished your case?

12.   What is the West reporter cite for the 2010 Second Circuit case that cited *Attia* for the point of law discussed in the eighth headnote?

13.   Click on the link for the case from Question 12. What is the name of the case in proper *Bluebook* format?

14.   Does the case involve a claim of reverse passing off under the Lanham Act or does it involve a claim of infringement under copyright?

ASSIGNMENT SEVEN
REVIEW—FINDING, CITING, AND UPDATING CASES
EXERCISE D

GOALS OF THIS ASSIGNMENT:
To review the use of Lexis Advance to find cases using headnotes and Shepard's.
To combine several steps of a research strategy using different types of materials.

You are working as a summer associate for the law firm of Jennings & Jennings in Annapolis, Maryland. Client Michael Peterson has retained the firm to review his Fourth Amendment claim. Last month, Mr. Peterson was on his sailboat on the Potomac River. During a routine check for appropriate life jackets, Coast Guard officers allegedly smelled the odor of marijuana and searched the boat finding drug paraphernalia, marijuana, and other illegal drugs. Mr. Peterson wants to know the chances of successfully suppressing this evidence from trial. You know that under the plain view exception to the warrant requirement, an officer can use all of his senses including his sense of smell. You have been asked to research **federal cases** concerning the constitutionality of **warrantless searches** other than those of a motor vehicle or occupant of a motor vehicle based on the **odor of marijuana**. Please conduct this research to determine how the court may deal with Mr. Peterson's situation. Before you begin, identify the federal jurisdiction that includes Maryland and determine which courts' cases will be mandatory authority in that jurisdiction.

Log on to Lexis Advance. If you need help navigating through Lexis Advance, please go back to the prior assignments to see specific instructions.

1. If you are unfamiliar with a topic and looking for citations to primary authority for your jurisdiction, a good place to begin your research is in the American Law Reports (A.L.R.). Search for an applicable A.L.R. Fed. annotation. What is the cite to the A.L.R. Fed. annotation?

   Find the 191 A.L.R. Fed. annotation.

2. What is the correct citation of the annotation itself? The annotation was published in 2004. (See Rule 16.7.6 of *The Bluebook*.)

3. Read section [11] (**Ships and boats**). What is the 1983 United States Court of Appeals, Fourth Circuit case cited? Provide the full West reporter citation to the case in correct format.

Click on the link for the case from Question 3 and read it.

4. Given your fact situation, is this case on point?

5. Is a United States Court of Appeals, Fourth Circuit case that is still good law mandatory or persuasive authority if cited to a federal district court in Maryland?

6. Look at the LexisNexis headnotes of this case. Several headnotes are relevant to your issue. Which headnote states that plain view encompasses more than simply seeing contraband, that for an object to be in plain view, it must only be obvious to the senses, and that odor alone is sufficient to place marijuana into plain view? List its number, e.g., first, second, third, etc.

7. What is the complete topic of this headnote from Question 6? Include all subtopics.

8. Read the text of the opinion corresponding to the headnote from Question 7. At this point in *Norman*, the court discusses *United States v. Sifuentes*. In *Sifuentes*, what did the cardboard boxes found in the impounded truck contain?

9.   Go back up to your LexisNexis headnote from Question 6. Provide the full West reporter citation to the United States Court of Appeals, Fourth Circuit case decided Nov. 30, 1981 assigned a headnote with the same topic from Question 7.

        Shepardize the case from Question 3.

10.   Does your case have any negative subsequent appellate history?

11.   What is the cite of the 2009 United States Court of Appeals, Fourth Circuit case that cited your case?

12.   What is the official reports cite of the entry for the 1993 United States Supreme Court case that cited *Norman* for the point of law discussed in LexisNexis headnote two?

13.   Click on the link for the case from Question 12. What is the name of the case in proper *Bluebook* format?

14.   Does the case ever mention an officer using his sense of smell to recognize the odor of marijuana?

ASSIGNMENT EIGHT
FINDING AND CITING STATUTES
EXERCISE A

GOALS OF THIS ASSIGNMENT:
To acquaint you with finding federal and state statutes in your library.
To familiarize you with the rules for citing statutes in *The Bluebook: A Uniform System of Citation*, 20th ed.

CITATION RULES: You will need to read and apply Bluepages B12 and Rule 12 (including its subsections) and review table T1 in *The Bluebook*. In this assignment, we give you either a citation or a subject area and you must find federal and state statutes. Once you have found the statutes, you must cite them correctly.

The first three questions require you to find and cite a statute in the official federal code, the *United States Code* (U.S.C.). The citation includes the title number, the code abbreviation, the section number(s), the date of the code appearing on the spine, and the supplement date (if the act appears in the supplement). Include the name of the act or the act's popular name and the original uncodified section of the act if such information would aid in identification. **Example: 26 U.S.C. § 420 (2012).**

1.   For statutes currently in force, which code should you cite?

2.   Find the U.S.C. in your library.

        a. What is the date of the current edition?

        b. What is the date of the latest supplement?

3.   Find and cite the *United States Code*, title 31, sections 301 to 310. Update in the latest supplement if needed. Do not include the name of the act.

The next question requires you to find and cite a statute in one of the unofficial federal codes, *United States Code Annotated* (U.S.C.A.). You may cite unofficial codes (U.S.C.A. and U.S.C.S.) when the statute is too recent to appear in the U.S.C. Include the information you used for the U.S.C., in addition to the name of the publisher. You must also include the precise location in either U.S.C.A. or U.S.C.S. where the statute appears. Cite to the main volume, the pocket part, or both. Since no date appears on the spine of the main volume, the year cited is the copyright date. **Example: 10 U.S.C.A. § 9344 (West 2010).**

4.   Find and cite § 7625 of Title 7 of U.S.C.A. correctly.

Next, you must find and cite a federal session law using *United States Statutes at Large*. According to Bluepages B12.1.1 and Rule 12.4 of *The Bluebook*, when citing session laws, always give the name of the statute; the public law number; the section number, if any; volume and page number of the Statutes at Large (Stat.); the year of passage if not revealed in its name; and codification information. **Example without codification information: Federal Trade Commission Improvements Act of 1980, Pub. L. No. 96-252, 94 Stat. 374.**

5.   Find and cite 109 Stat. 568. Do not include codification information.

For the next two questions, find and cite a state statute in a code. We require that you use the index to find the correct act. When citing a state code, include the name of the code; the chapter, title, or other subdivision; possibly the name of the publisher; and the year of the code. You must use table T1 to determine proper citation format for individual jurisdictions. **Example: Miss. Code Ann. § 75-5-109 (2002).**

6.   Use the index to the *Florida Statutes Annotated* and find the statute that creates the state's Council on Homelessness.

        For some states, most notably California, Texas, and New York, include the subject on the spine as part of the name of the code. **Example: Tex. Educ. Code Ann. § 11.058 (West 2012).**

7.   Use the index to the *Annotated California Code* and find a statute that deals with mud guards on motor vehicles.

ASSIGNMENT EIGHT
FINDING AND CITING STATUTES
EXERCISE B

GOALS OF THIS ASSIGNMENT:
To acquaint you with finding federal and state statutes in your library.
To familiarize you with the rules for citing statutes in *The Bluebook: A Uniform System of Citation,* 20th ed.

CITATION RULES: You will need to read and apply Bluepages B12 and Rule 12 (including its subsections) and review table T1 in *The Bluebook*. In this assignment, we give you either a citation or a subject area and you must find federal and state statutes. Once you have found the statutes, you must cite them correctly.

The first three questions require you to find and cite a statute in the official federal code, the *United States Code* (U.S.C.). The citation includes the title number, the code abbreviation, the section number(s), the date of the code appearing on the spine, and the supplement date (if the act appears in the supplement). Include the name of the act or the act's popular name and the original uncodified section of the act if such information would aid in identification. **Example: 26 U.S.C. § 420 (2012).**

1.   For statutes currently in force, which code should you cite?

2.   Find the U.S.C. in your library.

        a. What is the date of the current edition?

        b. What is the date of the latest supplement?

3.   Find and cite the *United States Code*, title 10, sections 161 to 166. Update in the latest supplement if needed. Do not include the name of the act.

The next question requires you to find and cite a statute in one of the unofficial federal codes, *United States Code Annotated* (U.S.C.A.). You may cite unofficial codes (U.S.C.A. and U.S.C.S.) when the statute is too recent to appear in the U.S.C. Include the information you used for the U.S.C., in addition to the name of the publisher. You must also include the precise location in either U.S.C.A. or U.S.C.S. where the statute appears. Cite to the main volume, the pocket part, or both. Since no date appears on the spine of the main volume, the year cited is the copyright date. **Example: 10 U.S.C.A. § 9344 (West 2010).**

4.   Find and cite § 1544 of Title 15 of U.S.C.A. correctly.

Next, you must find and cite a federal session law using *United States Statutes at Large*. According to Bluepages B12.1.1 and Rule 12.4 of *The Bluebook*, when citing session laws, always give the name of the statute; the public law number; the section number, if any; volume and page number of the Statutes at Large (Stat.); the year of passage if not revealed in its name; and codification information. **Example without codification information: Federal Trade Commission Improvements Act of 1980, Pub. L. No. 96-252, 94 Stat. 374.**

5.   Find and cite 115 Stat. 407. Do not include codification information.

For the next two questions, find and cite a state statute in a code. We require that you use the index to find the correct act. When citing a state code, include the name of the code; the chapter, title, or other subdivision; possibly the name of the publisher; and the year of the code. You must use table T1 to determine proper citation format for individual jurisdictions. **Example: Miss. Code Ann. § 75-5-109 (2002).**

6.   Use the index to the *West's Smith-Hurd Illinois Compiled Statutes Annotated* to find the statute that requires nail technicians to display their licenses.

        For some states, most notably California, Texas and New York, include the subject on the spine as part of the name of the code. **Example: Tex. Educ. Code Ann. § 11.058 (West 2012).**

7.   Use the index to the *Vernon's Texas Statutes and Codes Annotated* published by West and find the statute that prohibits the sale of lottery tickets to children.

ASSIGNMENT EIGHT
FINDING AND CITING STATUTES
EXERCISE C

GOALS OF THIS ASSIGNMENT:
To teach you how to find statutes in Westlaw.
To familiarize you with the rules for citing statutes in *The Bluebook: A Uniform System of Citation,* 20th ed.

CITATION RULES: You will need to read and apply Bluepages B12 and Rule 12 (including its subsections) and review table T1 in *The Bluebook.* In this assignment, we give you either a citation or a subject area and you must find federal and state statutes. Once you have found the statutes, you must cite them correctly. When citing to statutes on Westlaw, refer to Rule 18.3, Rule 12.5, and Rule 12.3.1(d).

   Sign on to Westlaw.

   Westlaw: If you are given the citation, retrieve your document by typing the citation into the search box. If the question asks you to search for a statute by subject, conduct a keyword search in **Illinois Statutes & Court Rules** for Questions 4 and 5, and **California Statutes & Court Rules** for Question 6.

   The first question requires you to retrieve and cite a statute in the *United States Code Annotated.* Westlaw retrieves U.S.C.A. The citation includes the title number, the code abbreviation, and the section number(s). The parenthetical includes the name of the publisher if needed, the name of the database, and the currency as given by the database. Include the name of the act or the act's popular name and the original uncodified section of the act if such information would aid in identification. Click on the **Currentness** link to access the date of the last update. **Example: 26 U.S.C.A. § 420 (West, Westlaw through xxxx).**

1.   Retrieve and cite the *United States Code Annotated,* title 43, section 617. Do not include the name of the act if the name is given. Refer to Rule 18.3, in addition to Rule 12.5, Rule 12.3.1(d), and table T1.

Next, you must retrieve and cite a federal session law from the *United States Statutes at Large*. According to Bluepages B12.1.1 and Rule 12.4 of *The Bluebook*, when citing session laws, always give the name of the statute; the public law number; the section number, if any; volume and page number of the Statutes at Large (Stat.); the year of passage if not revealed in its name; and codification information. **Example without codification information: Federal Trade Commission Improvements Act of 1980, Pub. L. No. 96-252, 94 Stat. 374.**

2.   Retrieve and cite 117 Stat. 624. Do not include codification information.

For the next four questions, retrieve and cite state statutes. Use Rule 18.3 which refers to Rule 12.5 to properly cite the statutes.

3.   Retrieve and cite Chapter 225, section 443/5 of the Illinois Statutes Annotated. For help with the proper search format for the citation, use the **find** template. From the Westlaw home page, click on **Statutes & Court Rules** under the All Content tab. Then click on **Illinois**. Next, click on the **Illinois Statutes Find Template** link under the **Tools & Resources** on the right.

4.   Search by keyword to retrieve the Illinois statute popularly known as the Degradable Plastic Act. Provide the proper citation to the **first section** (short title) of the law.

5.   Search by keyword to retrieve the Illinois statute stating that library circulation records are confidential. Provide the proper citation to the statute.

6.   Search by keyword to retrieve the California statute stating that the Director of Water Resources is appointed by the governor. Provide the proper citation to the statute.

ASSIGNMENT EIGHT
FINDING AND CITING STATUTES
EXERCISE D

GOALS OF THIS ASSIGNMENT:
To teach you how to find statutes in Lexis Advance.
To familiarize you with the rules for citing statutes in *The Bluebook: A Uniform System of Citation*, 20th ed.

CITATION RULES: You will need to read and apply Bluepages B12 and Rule 12 (including its subsections) and review table T1 in *The Bluebook*. In this assignment, we give you either a citation or a subject area and you must find federal and state statutes. Once you have found the statutes, you must cite them correctly. When citing to statutes on Lexis Advance, refer to Rule 18.3, Rule 12.5, and Rule 12.3.1(d).

Sign on to Lexis Advance.

Lexis Advance: If you are given the citation, retrieve your document by typing the citation into the search box. If the question asks you to search for a statute by subject, conduct a keyword search in the following for Questions 4 and 5: Content Type **Statutes and Legislation**, Content Type **Codes**, State **Indiana**, and General **In – Burns Indiana Statutes Annotated**. For Question 6, use Content Type **Statutes and Legislation**, Content Type **Codes**, State **California**, and General **CA – Deering's California Codes Annotated**.

The first question requires you to find and cite a statute in the *United States Code Service*. Lexis Advance retrieves U.S.C.S. The citation includes the title number, the code abbreviation, and the section number(s). The parenthetical includes the name of the publisher if needed, the name of the database, and the currency of the database. Include the name of the act or the act's popular name and the original uncodified section of the act if such information would aid in identification. The currency of the database for the code section is at the top of the statute. **Example: 26 U.S.C.S. § 420 (LexisNexis, LEXIS through xxxx).**

1.   Get and cite the *United States Code Service*, title 22, section 3945. Do not include the name of the act if the name is given. Refer to Rule 18.3, in addition to Rule 12.5, Rule 12.3.1(d), and table T1.

Next, you must find and cite a federal session law from the *United States Statutes at Large*. According to Bluepages B12 and Rule 12.4 of *The Bluebook*, when citing session laws, always give the name of the statute; the public law number; the section number, if any; volume and page number of the Statutes at Large (Stat.); the year of passage if not revealed in its name; and the codification information. **Example without codification information: Federal Trade Commission Improvements Act of 1980, Pub. L. No. 96-252, 94 Stat. 374.**

2.   Get and cite 117 Stat. 631. Do not include codification information.

For the next four questions, find and cite state statutes. Use Rule 18.3 which refers to Rule 12.5 to properly cite the statutes.

3.   Retrieve and cite section 31-14-6-3 of the Indiana Code Annotated.

4.   Search by keyword to retrieve the Indiana statute popularly known as the Indiana Abstract and Title Insurance Law. Provide the proper citation to the **first section** (Short title) of the law.

5.   Search by keyword to retrieve the Indiana statute defining the practice of addiction counseling for marriage and family therapists. Provide the proper citation to the statute.

6.   Search by keyword to retrieve the California statute stating that all patron use records of any public library are confidential. Provide the proper citation to the statute.

ASSIGNMENT NINE
FEDERAL CODES AND SESSION LAWS
EXERCISE A

GOALS OF THIS ASSIGNMENT:
To reveal the similarities and differences between the two annotated codes.
To introduce you to federal session laws.
To introduce you to the legislative history materials available in *United States Code Congressional and Administrative News.*

1.   Use the index in U.S.C.A. to find the title and section of the code to answer the following question. In elections for federal office where an individual has been permitted to provisionally vote at a polling place, the individual must execute a written affirmation before whom? Look up the section. Answer the question and provide the citation to the code. **Note**: In *The Bluebook*, use Bluepages B12, Rule 12 (including its subsections), and table T1.

2.   Continue with the law from Question 1. Look at the information in parentheses at the end of the text of the section in U.S.C.A. State the date, public law number, and *United States Statutes at Large* citation for the original 2002 act passed during the 107th Congress.

In your research, you will seldom, if ever, use the "official" U.S. Code, because it is not current and does not contain annotations. Therefore to answer Questions 3-7, use the two annotated codes, U.S.C.A. and U.S.C.S., of the code section you found in Question 1. **Be sure to check the pocket parts and the supplementary pamphlets for possible updates!**

3.   a.   Which code (U.S.C.A. and/or U.S.C.S.) provides cross references to other code sections within Title 52?
        b.   What sections of Title 52 U.S.C.S. are given?
                a.
                b.

4.   a.   Which codes (U.S.C.A. and/or U.S.C.S.) refer you to A.L.R. Fed. 2d annotations?

        b.   What is the cite of the annotation found in volume 47 of A.L.R. Fed. 2d?

               a.

               b.

5.   a.   Which code (U.S.C.A. and/or U.S.C.S.) refers you to topic and key numbers in the American Digest System?

        b.   List the **first listed** topic and its key numbers.

               a.

               b.

6.   a.   Which codes (U.S.C.A. and/or U.S.C.S.) refer you to court decisions?

        b.   State the **name** of the 2004 United States Court of Appeals, Sixth Circuit decision that generally interprets the statute.

               a.

               b.

7.   a.   Which code (U.S.C.A. and/or U.S.C.S.) refers you to treatises and practice aids?

        b.   What section of the *Americans with Disabilities: Practice and Compliance Manual* are you referred?

               a.

               b.

Reshelve the unofficial codes.

Remember that a code is a subject arrangement of current, general laws. Note how helpful the unofficial codes can be since they refer you to cases, encyclopedia articles, law review articles, digests, and secondary materials.

Now, assume that you want to look at the text of 116 Stat. 1706.

To find the text of a law or amendment as Congress passed it, use the *United States Statutes at Large* for Questions 8-11.

8.   Find 116 Stat. 1706. Go to the beginning of the Public Law at 116 Stat. 1666. What is the Public Law number?

9.   What is the bill number for the act?

10.   Examine the last page of the act. When was this act approved?

11.   What is the location of this volume in your library (indicate call number, row number, or other location)?

Now assume that you wish to see some legislative history for this act. Legislative history refers to committee reports, legislative debates, and hearings generated during the consideration of bills. Courts often consider legislative history when interpreting a statute because legislative history can show legislative intent.

For Questions 12 and 13, use *United States Code Congressional and Administrative News* (U.S.C.C.A.N.), an accessible source of legislative history and the text of public laws.

12.   The text of the public law you already examined in 116 Stat. is also reprinted in U.S.C.C.A.N. in 2002, vol. 2. Look it up. The **Legislative History** summary is located at the end of the text of your law. On what page of U.S.C.C.A.N. is the summary for your law's legislative history located?

13.   Look up the legislative history (it is in vol. 3). Which House Conference Report is reprinted?

ASSIGNMENT NINE
FEDERAL CODES AND SESSION LAWS
EXERCISE B

GOALS OF THIS ASSIGNMENT:
To reveal the similarities and differences between the two annotated codes.
To introduce you to federal session laws.
To introduce you to the legislative history materials available in *United States Code Congressional and Administrative News.*

1. Use the index in U.S.C.A. to find the title and section of the code to answer the following question. Usually the Office of Personnel Management has the authority to establish the maximum number of positions classified above GS-15 for an Executive Agency. Who has the authority to do so for a position above GS-15 in the Federal Bureau of Investigation? Look up the section. Answer the question and provide the citation to the code. **Note**: In *The Bluebook*, use Bluepages B12, Rule 12 (including its subsections), and table T1.

2. Continue with the law from Question 1. Look at the information in parentheses at the end of the section in the U.S.C.A. This law has been amended many times. State the date, public law number, and *United States Statutes at Large* citations for the 2009 amendment passed during the 111th Congress.

   In your research, you will seldom, if ever, use the "official" U.S. Code, because it is not current and does not contain annotations. Therefore to answer Questions 3-7, use the two annotated codes, U.S.C.A. and U.S.C.S., of the code section you found in Question 1. **Be sure to check the pocket parts and the supplementary pamphlets for possible updates!**

3. a. Which code (U.S.C.A. and/or U.S.C.S.) refers you to the Code of Federal Regulations?
   b. What is the cite to the C.F.R. provided?
      a.
      b.

4.   a.   Which code (U.S.C.A. and/or U.S.C.S.) refers you to A.L.R. Fed. annotations?

        b.   What is the cite of the annotation found in volume 72 of A.L.R. Fed.?

               a.

               b.

5.   a.   Which code (U.S.C.A. and/or U.S.C.S.) refers you to topic and key numbers in the American Digest System?

        b.   List the **first listed** topic and its key number.

               a.

               b.

6.   a.   Which codes (U.S.C.A. and/or U.S.C.S.) refer you to court decisions?

        b.   State the **name** of the 1975 United States Court of Claims decision interpreting this section.

               a.

               b.

7.   a.   Which code (U.S.C.A. and/or U.S.C.S.) refers you to treatises and practice aids?

        b.   What section of *West's Federal Administrative Practice* covers the topic Department of Labor – Office of the Solicitor?

               a.

               b.

Reshelve the unofficial codes.

Remember that a code is a subject arrangement of current, general laws. Note how helpful the unofficial codes can be since they refer you to cases, encyclopedia articles, law review articles, digests, and secondary materials.

Now, assume that you want to look at the text of 123 Stat. 2038.

To find the text of a law or amendment as Congress passed it, use the *United States Statutes at Large* for Questions 8-11.

8. Find 123 Stat. 2038. Go to the beginning of the Public Law at 123 Stat. 2023. What is the Public Law number?

9. What is the bill number for the act?

10. Examine the last page of the act. When was this act approved?

11. What is the location of this volume in your library (indicate call number, row number, or other location)?

Now assume that you wish to see some legislative history for this act. Legislative history refers to committee reports, legislative debates, and hearings generated during the consideration of bills. Courts often consider legislative history when interpreting a statute because legislative history can show legislative intent.

For Questions 12 and 13, use *United States Code Congressional and Administrative News* (U.S.C.C.A.N.), an accessible source of legislative history and the text of public laws.

12. The text of the public law you already examined in 123 Stat. is also reprinted in U.S.C.C.A.N. in 2009, vol. 2. Look it up. The **Legislative History** summary is located at the end of the text of your law. On what page of U.S.C.C.A.N. is the summary for your law's legislative history located?

13. Look up the legislative history (it is in vol. 3). Which House Conference Report is reprinted?

ASSIGNMENT NINE
FEDERAL CODES
EXERCISE C

GOALS OF THIS ASSIGNMENT:
To teach you statute searching on Westlaw.
To acquaint you with reading a federal code section on Westlaw.

Sign on to Westlaw.

These seven questions will ask you to locate a federal code section in U.S.C.A. and then answer questions about the code section.

Westlaw: Under All Content, select **Statutes & Court** Rules, then **United States Code Annotated (USCA)**. Conduct a keyword search. Your search may yield better results if your search contains Terms & Connectors.

1.   Search for the statute dealing with an agency's ability to pay a cash award to law enforcement officers who make substantial use of a foreign language in the performance of official duties. The award can be up to what percentage of basic pay? Answer the question and provide the citation to the code. In *The Bluebook*, use Rule 18.3, Rule 12.5, Rule 12.3.1(d), and table T1.

2.   How current is this section of the code? Click on **Currentness**.

3.   On what pages of the *United States Code Congressional and Administrative News* (U.S.C.C.A.N.) can you find the President's 1990 statement/message for the law from Question 1?
      Westlaw: Click on the **History** tab then click on **Legislative History Materials.** Scroll down to **Presidential Messages**.

4.   Westlaw allows you to link to the President's statement from Question 3 and read the full-text. Click on the link. Give the name of the President who made the statement.

5.   Return to the statute. What are the key numbers for the topic **United States** assigned to the subject of the statute?
        Westlaw: Click on the **Context & Analysis** tab and look at the **Library References**.

6.   What is the name of the 2005 United States Court of Federal Claims decision that cites the statute and discusses jurisdiction?
        Westlaw: Click on the **Citing References** tab and narrow your results to **Cases**.

7.   In addition to cases, does KeyCite provide citations to secondary sources that cite the statute?

ASSIGNMENT NINE
FEDERAL CODES
EXERCISE D

GOALS OF THIS ASSIGNMENT:
To teach you statute searching on Lexis Advance.
To acquaint you with reading a federal code section on Lexis Advance.

Sign on to Lexis Advance.

These seven questions will ask you to locate a federal code section in U.S.C.S. and then answer questions about the code section.

Lexis Advance: Conduct a keyword search in Content Type **Statutes and Legislation**, Content Type **Codes**, and Federal **USCS – United States Code Service – Titles 1 through 54**.Your search may yield better results if your search contains Terms & Connectors.

1. Search for the statute that provides the application of antitrust laws to professional major league baseball. Who has standing to sue under this section? Answer the question and provide the citation to the code. In *The Bluebook*, use Rule 18.3, Rule 12.5, Rule 12.3.1(d), and table T1.

2. How current is this section of the code?

3. Scroll down in this code section and look at the **History** section. This law was first enacted in 1914. In what year did Pub. L. No. 105-297 add this section?

4. What is the name of the law that was enacted as Pub. L. No. 105-297 that added this section?
   Lexis Advance: Scroll to the **Notes** section. Look at the information provided under **Other Provisions**.

5.   What is the title of the A.L.R. Fed. 2d annotation listed for this statute?
        Lexis Advance: Scroll down the **Research References & Practice Aids** section
        to see annotations.

6.   What is the name of the 2010 Eastern District of Wisconsin decision that cited
        this statute?
        Lexis Advance: Click on the **Shepardize this document** link on the right.

7.   In addition to cases, does Shepard's provide citations to secondary sources that
        cite the statute?
        Lexis Advance: Navigate to the **Other Citing Sources** report section to see if
        there are any secondary sources that cited the statute.

ASSIGNMENT TEN
FEDERAL LEGISLATIVE HISTORY ONLINE
EXERCISE A

GOAL OF THIS ASSIGNMENT:
To acquaint you with the ways to search for legislative history materials on Congress.gov, GPO's Federal Digital System (FDsys), ProQuest Congressional, and HeinOnline.

In this assignment, you will use two free legislative history websites, Congress.gov and GPO's Federal Digital System (FDsys) and two databases that are available by subscription, ProQuest Congressional and HeinOnline. You will have to check with your librarian to see if your library subscribes to the two subscription databases.

Before you begin working on Questions 1-9, you should read the information under the **About Congress.gov** link and the **About FDsys** link.

Questions 1-7 require you to use Congress.gov at **http://www.Congress.gov**. Congress.gov is the free official website maintained by the Library of Congress for accessing federal legislative documents, including bills, bill status, resolutions, committee reports, and issues of the *Congressional Record*. Congress.gov's strength is the integration of data and documents from many legislative sources.

We will begin searching the Curt Flood Act of 1998, Pub. L. No. 105-297. Access **Congress.gov**. Click on the **Public Laws** link under the heading **Bill Searches and Lists** on the Congress.gov homepage. On the next page, select 105 Congress (1997-1998) from the dropdown box. You now see a list of all public laws from the 105th Congress. Scroll down to PL 105-297.

Click on the public law **PL 105-297** link. Notice that the Senate bill number for our law is S. 63.

1.   Look at the overview. If the overview is not visible, click on the Show Overview link. Who is the main sponsor of the bill?

2.   Click on the **Actions** tab and select **ALL ACTIONS**. On 7/30/1998, the bill was laid before the Senate by unanimous consent as published in the *Congressional Record*. **Note**: "CR" stands for *Congressional Record*. List the page numbers where this appeared in the *Congressional Record*.

3.   Following from Question 2, click on *Congressional Record* page number link then the link for Curt Flood Act of 1997. Who asked for the unanimous consent to proceed to immediate consideration?

4.   Go back to the **All Actions** page for **S. 53**. What is the number of the report reported to the Senate on 10/29/1997?

5.   Click on the **Text** tab. Notice there are six version of the Senate bill as it went through the legislative process. To read the final version of the bill that became public law, have **Public Law (10/27/1998)** show in the version box. Click on the **PDF** link. You can cite to the public law as if you were citing to the original print source. Why? **Hint:** Read Rule 18.2.1(a)(i) in *The Bluebook*.

You can also search **Congress.gov** for bills that are not passed into law. Return to the Congress.gov homepage by clicking on **Congress.gov** which appears in the header at the top of every Congress.gov page.

6.   Search for a bill that was introduced in 2012, the Data Cap Integrity Act of 2012 (112th Congress). Click on the **Quick** search link at the top. Under **Choose Congresses**, select **112 (2011-2012)**. Under **Words/Phrases**, type the name of the act in the search box. Now click **Search**. Your result should locate S. 3703. Look at the information in the **Overview** box. To which Senate committee was the bill referred?

7.   Did the bill pass into law? **Hint**: Look at the Latest Action for this bill in the **Overview** box.

Next, you will use **GPO's Federal Digital System (FDsys)**, the Government Printing Office's website at **http://www.gpo.gov/fdsys**, to answer Questions 8 and 9. GPO's strength is providing free online versions of official federal government publications, including the *Congressional Record, Code of Federal Regulations*, *Federal Register*, and the *Compilation of Presidential Documents*. In addition, congressional documents, hearings, and reports are available, as well as public and private laws. FDsys offers PDF versions that retain the helpful formatting of the print originals.

8.   On the FDsys home page, click on the **About FDsys** link. On the right side of this page under **Quick Links > Authentication Info**, there is a **Be assured that publications from GPO web sites are official and authentic** link. Click this link and read the information. What does the digital signature, as viewed through the GPO Seal of Authenticity, verify?

9.   Go back to the FDsys home page. Under **Browse**, click on **Public and Private Laws**. Click on **112th Congress (2011-2012)** to expand. Click on **Public Law (Pub. L.)** to expand. Click on **0-99** to expand. Scroll to **Public Law 112-22** and click on its **PDF** link. What is the new designation of the United States Postal Service facility located at 4865 Tallmadge Road in Rootstown, Ohio?

Next, you will access **ProQuest Congressional** for Questions 10-13. This is a subscription database, so check your law library's list of databases and access it from the list or catalog.

The ProQuest Congressional database is very extensive and nicely arranged. It includes the full text of congressional publications, a bill tracking service, and the full text of public laws. Additional information includes a listing of Congressional members, committees, and political news. If you need help with this database, click on the **Congressional LibGuide** under **Help**. Click on the **How do I...** link under **Guide Contents**.

Again, we will search for the legislative history of the Curt Flood Act of 1998, Pub. L. No. 105-297. Using the ProQuest Congressional database, click on the **Advanced** search link. Click on Select all to unselect all document types. Select the document type **Legislative Histories**. In the top search box, type **PL 105-297**. Click **Search**.

Your results should give you the brief record for the legislative history for Pub. L. No. 105-297. Click on the title of the law to see the legislative history.

10. Is the full text of the act available as a link in the legislative history?

11. Examine the legislative history of Pub. L. No. 105-297. Under **Reports**, locate the listing for the report dated Oct. 29, 1997 from the First Session of the 105th Congress. Which Senate committee issued the report?

12. Go to the **Debates** section of the legislative history of Pub. L. No. 105-297. There are two references to the *Congressional Record*. What page of the *Congressional Record* indicates that the Senate considered and passed S. 53?

13. In the legislative history of Pub. L. No. 105-297, click on the link **Retrieve Bill Profile Report**. How many cosponsors of the bill were there?

Next, you will search **HeinOnline U.S. Federal Legislative History Library**. Check with your librarian to find out if your library subscribes to this database. It includes selective complete legislative histories on landmark acts. It also includes the finding aid based on Nancy P. Johnson's *Sources of Compiled Legislative Histories*. This source includes many law review articles and secondary materials on individual federal laws.

Access the **U.S. Federal Legislative History Library** on **HeinOnline**, and then click on **Sources of Compiled Legislative History Database** link at the top of the page.

14.   Under the **Search Sources of Compiled Legislative Histories Database** heading, use the dropdown to change Bill Number to **Public Law Number**. In the corresponding search box, type **110-289** and click **Search**. The result should be: **Public Law 110-289: Housing and Economic Recovery Act of 2008**. Click on the **Public Law 110-289** link. In what law review was Chad D. Emerson's article on this law published?

15.   On the same page, locate William H. Manz's publication on the Housing and Economic Recovery Act of 2008 and the Economic Stabilization Act of 2008. Which actual documents does the publication include?

HeinOnline U.S. Federal Legislative History Library also includes the **U.S. Federal Legislative History Title Collection**. Click on the link to that collection at the top of the page. The collection contains full-text legislative histories on some of the most important legislation.

16.   Find the entry for **Baseball and Antitrust: The Legislative History of the Curt Flood Act of 1998 Public Law No. 105-297, 112 Stat. 2824** in the list. Under **Cumulative Contents**, click on the **1 (Doc. Nos. 1-72, 2001)** link. Scroll down to locate the Senate Hearing 102-1094. Click on the link to open the document. Who was the first witness to testify at the hearing?

ASSIGNMENT TEN
FEDERAL LEGISLATIVE HISTORY ONLINE
EXERCISE B

GOAL OF THIS ASSIGNMENT:
To acquaint you with the ways to search for legislative history materials on Westlaw and Lexis Advance.

Sign on to Westlaw. Refer to Rule 18.3 on Commercial Electronic Databases and Rule 13.7 in *The Bluebook*.

Westlaw has extensive legislative history materials. There are several ways to access federal legislative histories; however, if you have a citation to a code section, you should begin your search for legislative history with *United States Code Annotated* on Westlaw.

Under **All Content**, click on **Statutes & Court Rules**. Next, click on the **United States Code Annotated (USCA)** link. You are seeking legislative history materials for the Curt Flood Act of 1998 whose Public Law number is Pub. L. No. 105-297. Type in **105-297** and you will retrieve several documents. Click on the link for **§ 26b. Application of the antitrust laws to professional major league baseball (15 U.S.C.A. § 26b)**. Scroll down to **CREDIT(S)**. The CREDITS indicate that the one of the amendments to this code section was Pub. L. No. 105-297 in 1998. Next, click on KeyCite's **History** tab at the top and then Legislative History Materials. This material may include citations to Proposed Legislation, Bill Drafts, Joint Committee Prints, *Congressional Record*, Testimony, and Presidential Messages. Use this information to answer Questions 1 and 2.

1. Congressional testimony is often difficult to locate on free websites. Fortunately, you can locate it on the commercial databases. Scroll to the Testimony section for Pub. L. No. 105-297. Click on the link for the **July 31, 1997 testimony**. This testimony was given for S. 53. Go to the beginning of the testimony. Who gave this statement?

2. Go back to your legislative history materials. Consult the **Congressional Record** section. On what date did the President approve the bill after sine die adjournment?

Westlaw also allows you to access directly the *Congressional Record*, which is a publication of the proceedings of United States Congress, including speeches, debates, and votes on the floor of the House and Senate.

Access the **Congressional Record**.

Westlaw: Click on **Legislative History** on All Content tab. Under Federal, click on **Congressional Record**.

Search for the "**Kate Puzey Peace Corps Volunteer Protection Act of 2011**." Include the quotation marks in your search. Use the results to answer Questions 3 and 4.

3.   Click on the entry that provides the text of a speech given on November 1, 2011 by a representative from California that was published in 157 Cong. Rec. E2014-04. Who gave the speech?

4.   Look at the top of the document. What is indicated as being included in the issue of the *Congressional Record*?

Westlaw also provides access to the *United States Code Congressional and Administrative News*. This publication contains the full text of public laws as well as selected committee reports relating to the public laws.

Access **U.S. Code Congressional & Administrative News (USCCAN)** and retrieve documents related to a specific act by using the name of the act as your search.

Westlaw: Click on **Legislative History** on All Content tab. Under Federal, click on **U.S. Code Congressional & Administrative News**.

Search for the "**Kate Puzey Peace Corps Volunteer Protection Act**." Include the quotation marks in your search. Use the results to answer Questions 5 and 6.

5.   In your search results, look at S. Rep. 112-82 dated Sept. 21, 2011. Which Senate committee issued this report?

6.   Who from the committee submitted the report from Question 5?

Westlaw offers thousands of federal legislative histories compiled by Government Accountability Office (GAO) law librarians. The coverage is between 1980 and 1995. The GAO legislative histories are very comprehensive.

Access the **U.S. GAO Federal Legislative Histories (FED-LH)** for Questions 7 and 8.

Westlaw: Click on **Legislative History** on All Content tab. Under Federal, click on **U.S. GAO Federal Legislative Histories**.

7.   Search for the **"Brady Handgun Violence Prevention Act"** including the quotation marks in your search. Notice the depth of legislative materials. Click on the United States Statutes at Large link (107 Stat. 1536). There is a great deal of information for this law. Go to the Presidential Documents section and click on the President's remarks on signing the Brady Bill. In his remarks, President Clinton states that the Brady Bill was first introduced almost 7 years earlier by which Ohio representative?

8.   Lastly, Westlaw saves your searches in reverse chronological order and allows you to access your previous content. On Westlaw, the feature is called **History** and is accessed by clicking on the **History** link at the top of the page. Access your History. Are you able to email this information to yourself?

Sign off Westlaw.

Next, sign on to **Lexis Advance.** Refer to Rule 18.3 on Commercial Electronic Databases and Rule 13.7 in *The Bluebook.*

Lexis Advance has a variety of sources available that allow you to search for legislative history materials. If you click on **Statutes and Legislation** under Content Type, you can then navigate to the **Legislative Histories** page, which contains a variety sources that can be selected and searched. You can also access the **Congressional Record** from the **Statutes and Legislation** page.

Let us return to the Kate Puzey Peace Corps Volunteer Protection Act and locate committee reports, debates, and the bill summary for Questions 9–11.

For Question 9, we will search Committee Reports. Under Content Type, click on **Statutes and Legislation**, then Content Type **Legislative Histories**, and then **Committee Reports**.

9. Conduct a search to retrieve reports for the Kate Puzey Peace Corps Volunteer Protection Act. Type **"Kate Puzey Peace Corps Volunteer Protection Act"** as your search and include the quotation marks in your search. What is the number of the Senate Report dated Sept. 21, 2011?

10. Return to **Statutes and Legislation** page. Click on **Congressional Record**. Search again for the **"Kate Puzey Peace Corps Volunteer Protection Act"** and include the quotation marks in your search. There are 14 results listed for the *Congressional Record.* Click on document **157 Cong. Rec. H 7178** from Nov. 1, 2011. Who moved to suspend the rules and pass S. 1280 to amend the Peace Corps Act?

11. Return to **Statutes and Legislation** page. Click on **Legislative Histories**, then **Federal Legislative Bill History**. Search again for the "Kate Puzey Peace Corps Volunteer Protection Act." There are 10 results listed. Click on document **2011 Legis. Bill Hist. US S.B. 1280** dated Nov. 21, 2011. This bill was enacted into law. What is the number of the Public Law?

Sign off Lexis Advance.

ASSIGNMENT ELEVEN
FINDING AND CITING ADMINISTRATIVE MATERIALS
EXERCISE A

GOALS OF THIS ASSIGNMENT:
To acquaint you with finding federal regulations and administrative decisions in your library.
To familiarize you with the rules for citing regulations and administrative decisions in *The Bluebook: A Uniform System of Citation*, 20th ed.

CITATION RULES: You will need to read Bluepages B14, Rules 14-14.3 (including subsections), and refer to tables T1.2, T6, T10.1, and T12. Apply these rules as you determine the correct citation for each regulation and decision. All of the materials in this assignment are U.S. government documents and may be shelved in the government documents area of your library.

The first question requires you to find and cite a regulation in the C.F.R. Cite all federal rules and regulations to the C.F.R. by title, section or part, and year. Include the name of the regulation if it is commonly known by its name. **Example: 7 C.F.R. § 1902.6 (2016).**

1. Find and cite the most recent edition of the *Code of Federal Regulations*, section 10.98 of Title 19. Do not include the name of the regulation.

The next question requires you to find and cite a regulation as originally printed in the daily *Federal Register*. Citations of regulations should give the commonly used name (if appropriate), the volume and page on which the regulation begins, and the exact date. When the *Federal Register* indicates where the rule will appear in the C.F.R., give that information in parentheses. **Example: 67 Fed. Reg. 49,599 (July 31, 2002) (to be codified at 38 C.F.R. pt. 20).**

2. Find the *Federal Register* for January 31, 2013 at page 6733 and cite the regulation correctly. Do not include the name of the regulation.

Next, you must find a proposed rule (that is, one that is not promulgated) in the *Federal Register* and cite it correctly. When citing proposed rules, follow the form for final rules (see above example), but also add the exact date it was proposed. **Example: 60 Fed. Reg. 3371 (proposed Jan. 17, 1995) (to be codified at 49 C.F.R. pt. 40).**

3.   Find the *Federal Register* for March 8, 2013 at page 14934 and cite it correctly. Do not include the name of the proposed regulation.

Now, find and cite an administrative decision or adjudication. When citing an administrative decision, cite by case name, report, and date - see Rule 14.3. The case name should only be the first-listed private party or subject-matter title. NOTE: If the case does not appear in an official agency reporter, then cite to a looseleaf service; see Rule 19 for details. **Example: *John Staurulakis, Inc.*, 4 F.C.C.R. 516 (1988).**

4.   Find the administrative decision involving Difco Laboratories, Inc. in volume 157 of the *Decisions and Orders of the National Labor Relations Board*. You may need to seek assistance from your librarian to locate administrative decisions in your library. Provide the full citation of the case.

The *Federal Register*, the C.F.R., and many administrative decisions are online on Westlaw and Lexis Advance, which you will use in the following assignment. You can also locate administrative materials on the Internet at http://www.nara.gov and http://www.gpo.gov/fdsys, as well as on the individual agencies' websites.

ASSIGNMENT ELEVEN
FINDING AND CITING ADMINISTRATIVE MATERIALS
EXERCISE B

GOALS OF THIS ASSIGNMENT:
To acquaint you with finding federal regulations and administrative decisions in your library.
To familiarize you with the rules for citing regulations and administrative decisions in *The Bluebook: A Uniform System of Citation*, 20th ed.

CITATION RULES: You will need to read Bluepages B14, Rules 14-14.3 (including subsections), and refer to tables T1.2, T6, T10.1, and T12. Apply these rules as you determine the correct citation for each regulation and decision. All of the materials in this assignment are U.S. government documents and may be shelved in the government documents area of your library.

The first question requires you to find and cite a regulation in the C.F.R. Cite all federal rules and regulations to the C.F.R. by title, section or part, and year. Include the name of the regulation if it is commonly known by its name. **Example: 7 C.F.R. § 1902.6 (2016).**

1.   Find and cite the most recent edition of the *Code of Federal Regulations*, section 1910.333 of Title 29. Do not include the name of the regulation.

The next question requires you to find and cite a regulation as originally printed in the daily *Federal Register*. Citations of regulations should give the commonly used name (if appropriate), the volume and page on which the regulation begins, and the exact date. When the *Federal Register* indicates where the rule will appear in the C.F.R., give that information in parentheses. **Example: 67 Fed. Reg. 49,599 (July 31, 2002) (to be codified at 38 C.F.R. pt. 20).**

2.   Find the *Federal Register,* for February 14, 2013 at page 10525 and cite the regulation correctly. Do not include the name of the regulation.

Next, you must find a proposed rule (that is, one that is not promulgated) in the *Federal Register* and cite it correctly. When citing proposed rules, follow the form for final rules (see above example), but also add the exact date it was proposed. **Example: 60 Fed. Reg. 3371 (proposed Jan. 17, 1995) (to be codified at 49 C.F.R. pt. 40).**

3.   Find the *Federal Register* for March 12, 2013 at page 15669 and cite it correctly. Do not include the name of the proposed regulation.

Now, find and cite an administrative decision or adjudication. When citing an administrative decision, cite by case name, report, and date - see Rule 14.3. The case name should only be the first-listed private party or subject-matter title. NOTE: If the case does not appear in an official agency reporter, then cite to a looseleaf service; see Rule 19 for details. **Example: *John Staurulakis, Inc.*, 4 F.C.C.R. 516 (1988).**

4.   Find the administrative decision involving Zalud Oldsmobile, Inc. in volume 113 of the *Federal Trade Commission Decisions*. You may need to seek assistance from your librarian to locate administrative decisions in your library. Provide the full citation of the case.

The *Federal Register*, the C.F.R., and many administrative decisions are online on Westlaw and Lexis Advance, which you will use in the following assignment. You can also locate administrative materials on the Internet at http://www.nara.gov and http://www.gpo.gov/fdsys, as well as on the individual agencies' websites.

ASSIGNMENT ELEVEN
FINDING AND CITING ADMINISTRATIVE MATERIALS
EXERCISE C

GOALS OF THIS ASSIGNMENT:
To acquaint you with finding federal regulations and administrative decisions on Westlaw.
To familiarize you with the rules for citing regulations and administrative decisions in *The Bluebook: A Uniform System of Citation*, 20th ed.

CITATION RULES: You will need to read Bluepages B14, Rules 14-14.3 (including subsections), and refer to tables T1, T6, T10.1, and T12. You also need to refer to Rule 18.3 and Rule 14.4 for citing regulations online.

Sign on to Westlaw.

Westlaw: Questions 1-6 provide you with enough information to retrieve your document by citation. Type the citation into the search box to retrieve the document.

1.   Retrieve and cite the most recent edition of the *Code of Federal Regulations*, section 241.7 of Title 33. Do not include the name of the regulation.

2.   Click on the **Currentness** link at the top of the regulation. How current on Westlaw is the regulation from Question 1?

The next question requires you to find and cite a regulation as originally printed in the daily *Federal Register*.

3.   Retrieve the *Federal Register,* vol. 78, for March 11, 2013 at page 15281 and cite the regulation correctly. Do not include the name of the regulation. **Note:** Westlaw added -01 to the page number in the citation to indicate that the regulation is either the first or only regulation on the page. Do not include -01 in the citation.

Next, you must find a proposed rule (that is, one that is not promulgated) in the *Federal Register* and cite it correctly.

4.   Retrieve the *Federal Register,* vol. 78, for January 3, 2013 at page 275 and cite it correctly. Do not include the name of the proposed regulation. **Note:** Westlaw added -01 to the page number in the citation to indicate that the regulation is either the first or only regulation on the page. Do not include -01 in the citation.

Next, find and cite an administrative decision or adjudication. When citing an administrative decision, cite by case name, report, and date - see Rule 14.3 including subsections. The case name should only be the first-listed private party or subject-matter title.

5.   Retrieve the administrative decision involving Samsonite Corporation, Inc. that begins on page 35 of volume 157 of the *Decisions and Orders of the National Labor Relations Board*. Provide the full citation of the decision. **Note:** For the abbreviation of the reporter, find the agency in Table T1.2.

6.   Retrieve the administrative decision involving Culligan, Inc. that begins on page 367 of volume 113 of the *Federal Trade Commission Decisions*. Provide the full citation of the decision. **Note:** For the abbreviation of the reporter, find the agency in Table T1.2.

ASSIGNMENT ELEVEN
FINDING AND CITING ADMINISTRATIVE MATERIALS
EXERCISE D

GOALS OF THIS ASSIGNMENT:
To acquaint you with finding federal regulations and administrative decisions on Lexis Advance.
To familiarize you with the rules for citing regulations and administrative decisions in *The Bluebook: A Uniform System of Citation*, 20th ed.

CITATION RULES: You will need to read Bluepages B14, Rules 14-14.3 (including subsections), and refer to tables T1, T6, T10.1, and T12. You also need to refer to Rule 18.3 and Rule 14.4 for citing regulations online.

Sign on to Lexis Advance.

Lexis Advance: Questions 1-6 provide you with enough information to retrieve your document by citation. Type the citation into the search box to retrieve the document. If you need help with the format for a citation, click on the **Get a Doc Assistance** link above the red search box.

1. Retrieve and cite the most recent edition of the *Code of Federal Regulations*, section 35.3500 of Title 40. Do not include the name of the regulation.

2. Look at the top of the regulation. How current on Lexis Advance is the regulation from Question 1?

The next question requires you to find and cite a regulation as originally printed in the daily *Federal Register*.

3. Retrieve the *Federal Register,* vol. 78, for February 4, 2013 at page 7674 and cite the regulation correctly. Do not include the name of the regulation.

Next, you must find a proposed rule (that is, one that is not promulgated) in the *Federal Register* and cite it correctly.

4.   Retrieve the *Federal Register,* vol. 78, for January 9, 2013 at page 1942 and cite it correctly. Do not include the name of the proposed regulation.

Next, find and cite an administrative decision or adjudication. When citing an administrative decision, cite by case name, report, and date - see Rule 14.3 including subsections. The case name should only be the first-listed private party or subject-matter title.

5.   Retrieve the administrative decision involving Furr's, Inc. that begins on page 387 of volume 157 of the *Decisions and Orders of the National Labor Relations Board*. Provide the full citation of the decision. **Note**: For the abbreviation of the reporter, find the agency in Table T1.2.

6.   Retrieve the administrative decision involving Roche Holding Ltd. that begins on page 1086 of volume 113 of the *Federal Trade Commission Decisions*. Provide the full citation of the decision. **Note**: For the abbreviation of the reporter, find the agency in Table T1.2.

ASSIGNMENT TWELVE
FEDERAL ADMINISTRATIVE RULES AND REGULATIONS
EXERCISE A

GOALS OF THIS ASSIGNMENT:
To develop your ability to find printed federal final regulations on a specific topic or issued pursuant to authority granted by a particular statute.
To update a regulation.
To search the C.F.R. and *LSA: List of Sections Affected* on the Internet.

To find the regulations for Questions 1-2, use the Index volume to the *Code of Federal Regulations* (most current year), published by the Government Printing Office. Use the print volumes of the sources to answer Questions 1-6. Refer to Bluepages B14 and Rule 14 (including subsections) in *The Bluebook*. When citing a regulation, omit the name from the citation.

1.   Using the Parallel Table of Authorities and Rules in the Index volume. By using this table you can find regulations that were adopted under the authority of a specific title and section of the U.S.C. Locate which title and part of the C.F.R. were adopted under the authority of **7 U.S.C. § 1524**. Find the answer in the C.F.R. State the citation in proper format.

2.   Now, use the CFR Index in the same Index volume. Find and cite the regulations concerning the requirements for bunk beds.

    Reshelve the Index volume.

3.   Find the text of the regulation part from the previous question. What is the statutory authority for the regulation part? State the reference to the U.S.C. found in the Authority note.

4.   Where was the first section of the part in Question 2 originally published in the *Federal Register*? State the source note as printed in the C.F.R.

To update the C.F.R. use the slim pamphlet, *LSA: List of CFR Sections Affected*. In real-life research, you would use the most recent monthly issue. However, for practice purposes, you will use a designated issue. Use the *LSA: List of CFR Sections Affected* to answer Questions 5 and 6.

5. Using the *LSA: List of CFR Sections Affected*, March 2016, determine if any change occurred in 21 C.F.R. § 640.14. What is the status of that section?

6. Where would you find this change in the 2015 *Federal Register*?

    Use the Internet to answer Questions 7 and 8.

7. Repeat Question 2 using the e-CFR website at http://www.ecfr.gov. This website is an editorial compilation of C.F.R. material and *Federal Register* amendments. It is updated daily. What search terms did you use to retrieve the regulation? **Hint**: When performing the search, use the **Boolean** search link under **Advanced Search** on the left. Look for your regulation in the search results.

8. Repeat Question 5 using GPO's Federal Digital System website at http://www.gpo.gov/fdsys. Under **Browse**, click on **Code of Federal Regulations**. Scroll down and click on **List of CFR Sections Affected** on the left. Expand **Monthly LSA**. Expand **2016**. Expand **January**. Scroll down to your title and click the PDF link on the right. Find the regulation in the list. Did you find the same answer to Question 5?

ASSIGNMENT TWELVE
FEDERAL ADMINISTRATIVE RULES AND REGULATIONS
EXERCISE B

GOALS OF THIS ASSIGNMENT:
To develop your ability to find printed federal final regulations on a specific topic or issued pursuant to authority granted by a particular statute.
To update a regulation.
To search the C.F.R. and *LSA: List of Sections Affected* on the Internet.

To find the regulations for Questions 1-2, use the Index volume to the *Code of Federal Regulations* (most current year), published by the Government Printing Office. Use the print volumes of the sources to answer Questions 1-6. Refer to Bluepages B14 and Rule 14 (including subsections) in *The Bluebook*. When citing a regulation, omit the name from the citation.

1.   Using the Parallel Table of Authorities and Rules in the Index volume. By using this table you can find regulations that were adopted under the authority of a specific title and section of the U.S.C. Locate which title and part of the C.F.R. were adopted under the authority of **10 U.S.C. § 826**. Find the answer in the C.F.R. State the citation in proper format.

2.   Now, use the CFR Index in the same Index volume. Find and cite the regulations concerning executive clemency.

Reshelve the Index volume.

3.   Find the text of the regulation part from the previous question. What is the authority for the regulation part? State the references to the United States Constitution and the U.S.C. found in the Authority note.

4.   Where did the first section of the part in Question 2 appear in the *Federal Register*? State the source note as printed in the C.F.R.

> To update the C.F.R. use the slim pamphlet, *LSA: List of CFR Sections Affected*. In real-life research, you would use the most recent monthly issue. However, for practice purposes, you will use a designated issue. Use the *LSA: List of CFR. Sections Affected* to answer Questions 5 and 6.

5. Using the *LSA: List of CFR Sections Affected*, February 2016, determine if any change occurred in 19 C.F.R. § 10.69. What is the status of that section?

6. Where would you find this change in the 2015 *Federal Register*?

Use the Internet to answer Questions 7 and 8.

7. Repeat Question 2 using the e-CFR website at http://www.ecfr.gov. This website is an editorial compilation of C.F.R. material and *Federal Register* amendments. It is updated daily. What search terms did you use to retrieve the regulation? **Hint**: When performing the search, use the **Boolean** search link under **Advanced Search** on the left. You may have to scroll down the page to find the regulation.

8. Repeat Question 5 using GPO's Federal Digital System website at http://www.gpo.gov/fdsys. Under **Browse**, click on **Code of Federal Regulations**. Scroll down and click on **List of CFR Sections Affected** on the left. Expand **Monthly LSA**. Expand **2016**. Expand **February**. Scroll down to your title and click the PDF link on the right. Find the regulation in the list. Did you find the same answer to Question 5?

ASSIGNMENT TWELVE
FEDERAL ADMINISTRATIVE RULES AND REGULATIONS
EXERCISE C

GOALS OF THIS ASSIGNMENT:
To locate codified regulations on Westlaw.

Sign on to Westlaw.

Westlaw: On the **All Content** tab, click on **Regulations**. Then click on **Code of Federal Regulations (CFR)** under **Federal**.

Refer to Bluepages B14, Rule 14 (including subsections), and Rule 18.3 in *The Bluebook*. When citing a regulation, omit the name from the citation.

1.   Use a keyword search to find regulations providing that discrimination is prohibited against the handicapped in federally assisted programs of the Department of Commerce. In your results, click on the regulation titled **Discrimination prohibited** found in the C.F.R. title covering **Commerce and Foreign Trade.** Provide the citation to the C.F.R. for this regulation.

2.   Examine regulation § 8b.4. What is the statutory authority for the regulation? Provide the reference to the U.S.C. as displayed in the Authority note after the text of the regulation.

3.   How current is this regulation?

4.   On Westlaw, is it necessary to update a C.F.R. citation using the *Federal Register*?

5.   Next, go to cases under **KeyCite's Citing References** tab at the top. What is the name of the 1985 Supreme Court of the United States decision that cites this regulation?

6.   Does KeyCite provide citations to the *Federal Register* for this regulation? Look under **Administrative Decisions & Guidan**ce on the **Citing References** tab.

7.   If there are prior versions of your regulation, Westlaw allows you to see these versions. To do so, click on KeyCite's **History** tab and then on **Versions**. In research, what would be the value of an earlier edition of the C.F.R.?

ASSIGNMENT TWELVE
FEDERAL ADMINISTRATIVE RULES AND REGULATIONS
EXERCISE D

GOALS OF THIS ASSIGNMENT:
To locate codified regulations on Lexis Advance.

Sign on to Lexis Advance.

Lexis Advance: Select Content Type **Administrative Codes and Regulations**, Content Type **Administrative Codes**, and Federal **CFR – Code of Federal Regulations**.

Refer to Bluepages B14, Rule 14 (including subsections), and Rule 18.3 in *The Bluebook*. When citing a regulation, omit the name from the citation.

1.   Use a keyword search to find regulations providing for nondiscrimination in financial assistance programs of the Small Business Administration. In your results, click on the regulation titled **Discrimination prohibited** found in the C.F.R. title covering Business Credit and Assistance. Provide the citation to the C.F.R. for this regulation.

2.   Examine regulation § 113.3. What is the statutory authority for the regulation? Provide the references to title 15 of the U.S.C. as displayed in the Authority note after the text of the regulation.

3.   Examine the History note at the end of your regulation. What is the cite to the *Federal Register* where the regulation was published on Apr. 4, 1979?

4.   How current is this regulation?

5.   On Lexis Advance, is it necessary to update a C.F.R. citation suing the *Federal Register*?

6.   Shepardize the regulation. What is the name of the 1982 Supreme Court of the United States decision that cites this regulation?

7.   Does Shepard's provide citations to the *Federal Register* for this regulation?

ASSIGNMENT THIRTEEN
REVIEW—FINDING STATUTES AND REGULATIONS
EXERCISE A

GOALS OF THIS ASSIGNMENT:
To review statutory and regulatory research.
To require you to use statutes, legislative history, and regulations to solve research problems.

You are clerking for a law firm during the summer. Your supervising attorney has a client whose third-grade son's public elementary school is holding a mother-daughter tea. The client believes that this mother-daughter tea violates the federal law that prohibits educational institutions that receive federal funding from discriminating based on sex. The lawyer wants you to research if the public elementary school can hold a mother-daughter activity without violating the federal law that prohibits discrimination based on sex in education. You begin your research with the federal annotated code since the question involves a federal law.

1. Use the Index to U.S.C.A. to determine the appropriate code section. Look up the act and answer Questions 1-6.

   a. What is the correct citation to the code section that deals with whether a public school may hold a mother-daughter tea without violating the federal law that prohibits discrimination based on sex in education?

   b. Read the code section. May a public elementary school hold a mother-daughter event without violating the federal law?

2. Examine the section. What is the Public Law number of the 1972 act?

3. Under **Library References**, what is the West topic and key number for cases concerning this subject?

167

4.   Under **Historical and Statutory Notes**, find the reference to the legislative history of the 1972 act. Look at the citation to U.S.C.C.A.N. On what page of the 1972 U.S.C.C.A.N. does the legislative history's House Report begin?

5.   This statute has a related federal regulation. Where in the C.F.R. do you find regulations dealing with the policies and procedures generally?

6.   Next, examine the **Notes of Decisions**. Find a 1993 District of Colorado decision where the court indicated a financial crisis is not a **justification** for gender discrimination under Title IX. What is the name of the case?

Reshelve U.S.C.A. and find U.S.C.C.A.N.

7.   Examine the legislative history in the 1972 U.S.C.C.A.N. from Question 4. Which House Report is reprinted in U.S.C.C.A.N.?

Reshelve U.S.C.C.A.N. and find the C.F.R.

8.   Look up the regulations from Question 5 in the C.F.R. Read the specific section that provides definitions. The word "Department" means which department?

ASSIGNMENT THIRTEEN
REVIEW—FINDING STATUTES AND REGULATIONS
EXERCISE B

GOALS OF THIS ASSIGNMENT:
To review statutory and regulatory research.
To require you to use statutes, legislative history, and regulations to solve research problems.

You are clerking for a law firm during the summer. Your supervising attorney has a client who is the director of the local community theater. The client wants his theater troupe to perform a play with a military theme. Consequently, his actors will need to wear military uniforms. The client wants to know if there are any laws that would prohibit actors from wearing uniforms of the armed forces in a stage production. Please research this issue. You will begin your research with the federal annotated code since the question involves a federal law.

1.   Use the Index to U.S.C.A. to determine the appropriate code section. Look up the act and answer Questions 1-6.

      a.   What is the correct citation to the code section concerning persons not on active duty, such as actors, wearing uniforms of the armed forces?

      b.   Read the code section. May an actor in a theatrical production who is portraying a member of the armed forces wear the uniform for that armed force?

2.   Examine the section. What is the Public Law number of the 1996 act?

3.   Under **Library References**, what are the West topic and two key numbers for cases concerning this subject?

169

4. Under **Historical and Statutory Notes**, find the reference to the legislative history of the 1996 act. Look at the citation to U.S.C.C.A.N. On what page of the 1996 U.S.C.C.A.N. does the legislative history's House Report begin?

5. This statute has a related federal regulation. Where in the C.F.R. do you find regulations concerning the limitations on wearing a uniform?

6. Next, examine the **Notes of Decisions**. Find a 1970 Supreme Court of the United States decision that held that the section of the law (f) permitting an actor in a theatrical production to wear a uniform in portraying a member of an armed force if the portrayal does not tend to discredit that armed force must be stricken to preserve the constitutionality of the remainder of the law. What is the name of the case?

Reshelve U.S.C.A. and find U.S.C.C.A.N.

7. Examine the legislative history in the 1996 U.S.C.C.A.N. from Question 4. Which House Report (not conference report) is reprinted in U.S.C.C.A.N.?

Reshelve U.S.C.C.A.N. and find the C.F.R.

8. Look up the regulations from Question 5 in the C.F.R. Under the regulation providing policy, may a member of the Armed Forces wear his uniform while he participates in a picket line unauthorized by competent Service authority?

ASSIGNMENT THIRTEEN
REVIEW—FINDING STATUTES AND REGULATIONS
EXERCISE C

GOALS OF THIS ASSIGNMENT:
To review statutory and regulatory research on Westlaw.
To require you to use statutes, legislative history, and regulations to solve research problems.

You are clerking for a criminal defense law firm during the summer. Your supervising attorney has a client who was indicted for distributing cocaine with the knowledge or intent that the controlled substance be unlawfully imported into the United States. To prepare a defense, the attorney has asked you to research whether or not the statute requires actual knowledge or simply constructive knowledge that the controlled substance will be unlawfully imported into the United States. You will begin your research with the federal annotated code since the question involves a federal law.

Sign on to Westlaw. If you need help navigating through Westlaw, please go back to the prior assignments to see specific instructions.

1. Conduct a search to find the United States Code Annotated section that discusses the distribution of a controlled substance for the purpose of unlawful importation into the United States. Click on the section and answer Questions 1–8.

    a. What is the correct citation to the code section?

    b. What drugs fall under this law?

2. How current is this section of the code?

3. Examine the section. What is the Public Law number of the 1970 act?

4.   What is the West topic and key numbers for cases concerning this subject?

5.   Find the **Historical and Legislative Reports** under the **Editor's and Revisor's Notes** in the **History** tab. Look for the congressional reports (part of legislative history) the for the 1970 act. What is the cite to the House Report listed?

6.   Click on the link to the House Report for the 1970 act. What is the date of the House Report?

7.   This statute has related federal regulations. Locate the references to the C.F.R.

   a.   Where in the C.F.R. do you find regulations on the availability of information on drug control policy?

   b.   Click on the link to the C.F.R. The purpose of the regulations in this part is to set rules about publicly available information related to the Office of National Drug Control Policy under what law?

8.   Next, examine the **Notes of Decisions**. Find a 2009 United States Court of Appeals, Second Circuit decision where the court held that the government must prove beyond a reasonable doubt that the defendant had actual knowledge or intent that the controlled substance would be imported into the United States. What is the name of the case?

ASSIGNMENT THIRTEEN
REVIEW—FINDING STATUTES AND REGULATIONS
EXERCISE D

GOALS OF THIS ASSIGNMENT:
To review statutory and regulatory research on Lexis Advance.
To require you to use statutes, legislative history, and regulations to solve research problems.

You are clerking for a law firm during the summer. Your supervising attorney has a client who wants to know how to get a certificate of citizenship for her children who were born outside the United States and are residing outside the United States. The client has not been a member of the armed forces and her children were not adopted. The lawyer wants you to research how to acquire such a certificate of citizenship. You begin your research with the federal annotated code since the question involves a federal law.

Sign on to Lexis Advance. If you need help navigating through Lexis Advance, please go back to the prior assignments to see specific instructions.

1. Conduct a search to find the appropriate United States Code Service section that addresses how to obtain a certificate of citizenship for children born and residing outside the United States. Look up the act and answer Questions 1-8.

    a. What is the correct citation to the code section?

    b. Under this section, which government official issues the certificate of citizenship?

2. How current is this section of the code?

3. Examine the law. What is the Public Law number of the 2002 act?

173

4. What sections of the Am. Jur. 2d topic Aliens and Citizens are relevant to this law?

5. Where would you find **Code of Federal Regulations** sections related to the Department of Homeland Security and the subject of your research?

6. Look at the decisions interpreting the section. Find a 2008 United States Court of Appeals, Ninth Circuit decision where the court held that the government was not estopped from denying citizenship to a lawful, permanent resident who had been charged with removability because he was an alien who committed an aggravated felony and he had failed to comply with the statutory requirements to become a naturalized citizen. What is the name of the case?

7. **Shepardize** the United States Code Service section. Locate the 1961 United States Supreme Court decision that cited this law. What is the name of the case?

8. Look at the **History** report section of your Shepard's display. What is the cite to the law in the *United States Statutes at Large* that amended this code section in 2008?

ASSIGNMENT FOURTEEN
SECONDARY AUTHORITY
EXERCISE A

GOALS OF THIS ASSIGNMENT:

To familiarize you with one of two major legal encyclopedias and your state legal encyclopedia.

To introduce you to a legal periodical index/database and how to cite legal periodical articles – in either print or online.

To show you how to find treatises in your library.

To introduce you to looseleaf services in print.

Answer Questions 1-2 using *American Jurisprudence 2d.*

1. Begin in the Index volumes. Provide the complete citation of the section that deals with employment authorization at the Library of Congress for aliens. Use *Bluebook* form, Bluepages B15.1 and Rule 15.8(a).

2. Look up the section. This section indicates that a maximum of 15 positions in the Library of Congress are exempt from appropriation Acts provisions concerning the employment of aliens during a current fiscal year. What is the United States Code Annotated provision that is cited for this proposition?

3. Does your state have a legal encyclopedia? If so, state the title of the encyclopedia.

To answer Questions 4 and 5, use either *HeinOnline: Law Journal Library* or *Index to Legal Periodicals & Books* in print. Refer to Bluepages B16, Rule 16, and table T13. Look at the actual articles to cite them.

4. Provide the complete citation to a 2009 article concerning animal cruelty and crush videos.

5. State the citation of the June 2008 article authored by Stephanie Francis Ward that appeared in the *ABA Journal* on lawyers writing for television. **Note**: This journal is not consecutively paged, so follow Bluepages B16.1.2 and Rule 16.5. **Tip**: If there is a subtitle, do not include it.

6. If your law library holds this issue, where is this periodical in your library? Provide either a row number or call number.

    You should use your library's online catalog to answer questions 7 and 8.

7. Find the 2011 hornbook on federal courts by Charles Alan Wright and Mary Kay Kane in your library. Cite it according to Bluepages B15 and Rule 15.

8. Find the 2012 nutshell on arbitration by Thomas E. Carbonneau. Provide the call number or location of the book in your library.

Answer questions 9 and 10 using *Uniform Commercial Code Reporting Service*, Second Series in print.

9. Locate the FINDEX volume of the *Uniform Commercial Code Reporting Service, Second Series*. Use the Cumulative Findex Supplement, a table that indexes, using the appropriate paragraph numbers, cases and commentary material printed in volumes (beginning with 28) of the UCC Reporting Service 2d. The paragraph numbers are keyed to the corresponding sections of the Uniform Commercial Code (UCC). For example, ¶1102 in the table corresponds to § 1-102 of the UCC. Provide the citation as it appears in the table to the case in the UCC Reporting Service 2d involving § 2-313 of the U.C.C. dealing with express warranties and advertising of cereal.

10. Find the decision from question 9 in volume 69 of the UCC Reporting Service 2d. State the name of the 2009 decision from the United States District Court, Eastern District of California where the buyer of cereal brought a breach-of-express-warranty claim alleging the manufacturer warranted that a cereal contained real fruit when the cereal contained only "Crunchberries," which are not real fruit.

ASSIGNMENT FOURTEEN
SECONDARY AUTHORITY
EXERCISE B

GOALS OF THIS ASSIGNMENT:
To familiarize you with the two major legal encyclopedias and your state legal encyclopedia.
To introduce you to a legal periodical index/database and how to cite legal periodical articles, in either print or online.
To show you how to find treatises in your library.
To introduce you to looseleaf services in print.

Answer Questions 1-2 using *American Jurisprudence 2d.*

1. Begin in the Index volumes. Provide the complete citation to the section that discusses the educational fair use doctrine under copyright. Use *Bluebook* form, Bluepages B15.1 and Rule 15.8(a).

2. Look up the section. This section indicates that the fair-use provision of the Copyright Act of 1976 refers to the reproduction of multiple copies for classroom use and provides that the purpose and character of the use are factors to be considered in determining fair use. What is the United States Code Annotated provision that is cited for this proposition?

3. Does your state have a legal encyclopedia? If so, state the title of the encyclopedia.

To answer Questions 4 and 5, use either *HeinOnline: Law Journal Library* or *Index to Legal Periodicals & Books* in print. Refer to Bluepages B16, Rule 16, and table T13. Look at the actual articles to cite them.

4.   Provide the complete citation to a 2008 article on cigarette advertising and toxic tort law.

5.   State the citation of the August 2009 article authored by Stephanie Francis Ward on the greatest legal television shows that appeared in the *ABA Journal*. **Note**: This journal is not consecutively paged, so follow Bluepages B16.1.2 and Rule 16.5.

6.   If your law library holds the issue from Question 5, where is this periodical in your library? Provide either a row number or call number.

        You should use your library's online catalog to answer questions 7 and 8.

7.   Find the 2008 hornbook on products liability law by David G. Owen in your library. Cite it according to Bluepages B15 and Rule 15.

8.   Find the 2012 nutshell on pretrial litigation by R. Lawrence Dessem. Provide the call number or location of the book in your library.

Answer questions 9 and 10 using *CCH Standard Federal Tax Reporter* in print.

9. Look in the topical index and find the paragraph number that examines whether a member of the clergy can deduct expenses for his automobile as a business expense. What is the paragraph number?

10. Browse the text of the answer from Question 9. What is the number of the Revenue Ruling that stated that a minister who undertook his duties without compensation and without a profit motive was not engaged in a trade or business so that his automobile expenses incurred while carrying out his ministerial duties were not deductible as business expenses?

ASSIGNMENT FOURTEEN
SECONDARY AUTHORITY
EXERCISE C

GOALS OF THIS ASSIGNMENT:
To familiarize you with *American Jurisprudence 2d* on Westlaw.
To teach you how to find periodical articles on Westlaw.
To introduce you to a looseleaf service online.

Sign on to Westlaw.

Answer questions 1-2 using the *American Jurisprudence 2d*.

Westlaw: Under **All Content**, select **Secondary Sources**, then select **Texts & Treatises**, and then select **American Jurisprudence 2d**.

1. Search for the entry that discusses the ownership of airspace over property. What is the Am. Jur. 2d topic and section number?

2. Read the section. The section indicates a landowner's property interest in land extends to the airspace directly over the property, to the extent that the airspace can be used to benefit the underlying land. This statement is supported by case law. What is the name of the 1995 United States Court of Federal Claims decision that was affirmed the following year by the United States Court of Appeals, Federal Circuit?

    To answer Questions 3-5, you will access law reviews and journals. Refer to Bluepages B16, Rule 16, 18.3, Rules 16.8, and table T13.

    Westlaw: Under **All Content**, select **Secondary Sources**, then select **Law Reviews & Journals**.

3. Search for the 2008 Tulane Law Review article about New Orleans, Katrina, and *Kelo*. Provide the citation to the article. The unique Westlaw identifier for your citation is at the end of the article.

4.   Does Westlaw contain the full-text of law review article in Question 3?

5.   Look at KeyCite's **Citing References** for this article. What is the name of the 2009 Louisiana decision that cited the article?

Answer question 6 using *Immigration Law Service 2d*.

Westlaw: Under **All Content**, select **Secondary Sources**. Scroll down to **By Topic**, select **Immigration**, then **Immigration Law Service 2d** under **Texts & Treatises**. Select **Immigration Law Service 2d** on the next screen.

6.   Locate the section that discusses generally the availability of nonimmigrant visas under which foreign nationals may come to the United States to study. What is the section?

ASSIGNMENT FOURTEEN
SECONDARY AUTHORITY
EXERCISE D

GOALS OF THIS ASSIGNMENT:
To familiarize you with *American Jurisprudence 2d* **on Lexis Advance.**
To teach you how to find periodical articles on Lexis Advance.
To introduce you to a looseleaf service online.

> **Sign on to Lexis Advance.**
>
> **Answer questions 1-2 using the** *American Jurisprudence 2d* **source.**
>
> **Lexis Advance:** Under **Content Type**, click on **Secondary Materials** and then **American Jurisprudence 2d (AMJUR)** under **Content Type Federal**.

1. Search for the entry that deals with the test of confidentiality of trade secrets under the Freedom of Information Act. What is the Am. Jur. 2d topic and section number?

2. Read the section. The section states that the test for determining confidentiality of a trade secret where the information sought was not voluntarily submitted to the government may also apply under a comparable state act. What is the name of the 2004 case that is cited for this proposition?

> **To answer Questions 3-5, you will access law reviews and journals. Refer to Bluepages B16, Rule 16, 18.3, Rules 16.8, and table T13.**

3. Provide the citation to the 2012 Harvard Law Review article discussing the core meaning of the suspension clause.
    Lexis Advance: Under **Content Type**, select **Secondary Materials** and then Content Type **Law Reviews & Journals**.

4.   Does Lexis Advance contain the full-text of the law review article in Question 3?

5.   Shepardize this article. Look at the citing decision. What is the name of the 2013 Unites States Court of Appeals, Tenth Circuit decision that cited the article?

Answer question 6 using Matthew Bender's *Federal Income, Gift and Estate Taxation* on Lexis Advance.

Lexis Advance: Under **Content Type**, click on **Secondary Materials**, then on Content Type **Treatises, Practice Guides & Jurisprudence**. Scroll down to **Practice Area** and click on **Estate, Gift & Trust Law**. Scroll down and select **Federal Income, Gift and Estate Taxation**.

6.   Conduct a search for the section dealing with the deduction of business expenses which has an interpreting decision disallowing a teacher from deducting the cost of comic books used in after school activities. Select to view the section that discusses personal versus business expenses. Click on footnote 104. Link to the Tax Court decision in the footnote. On what date was the decision filed?

ASSIGNMENT FIFTEEN
REVIEW—FINDING SECONDARY AUTHORITY
EXERCISE A

GOALS OF THIS ASSIGNMENT:
To review the use of sources of secondary authority.
To emphasize how the various publications cross-reference users to other materials.

Logan Bradford and Casey Davidson have hired the Ohio law firm for which you are clerking to represent them. Logan and Casey are same-sex partners who want to jointly adopt a child. The couple wants to know if domestic partners are permitted jointly to adopt a child who is not biologically related to either of them.

The attorney assigned to Logan and Casey's case has asked you to conduct some preliminary research on the issue of whether a same-sex couple may petition jointly to adopt a child who is not biologically related to either party.

1. Into what broad areas of the law does this question fall?

2. Using your online library catalog, find a treatise in your library on adoption law. List the author, title, and date of publication.

3. Use either *HeinOnline: Law Journal Library* or *Index to Legal Periodicals & Books* in print. Find a 2011 law review article concerning constitutional challenges to same-sex adoption. The article appeared in the **Capital University Law Review**. Find the article in your library and cite it using proper *Bluebook* form.

4. Another good source of secondary authority is A.L.R. Use the A.L.R. Index to find an A.L.R.6th annotation published in 2011 on Logan and Casey's issue of same-sex partners jointly adopting a child. Look up the annotation and provide the citation using proper *Bluebook* form. **Tip:** Newer annotations are indexed in the pocket part.

5. Now examine the beginning of the A.L.R. annotation. Note the different types of cross references to other publications and related annotations. Under what sections of Am. Jur. 2d topic *Adoption* do you find information related to this topic?

6. *American Jurisprudence 2d* may also provide background information on an area of unfamiliar law. Find the topic *Adoption* in Am. Jur. 2d in your library. Read § 131 and answer the following question. What do the adoptive parents have the burden of proving by clear and convincing evidence?

ASSIGNMENT FIFTEEN
REVIEW—FINDING SECONDARY AUTHORITY
EXERCISE B

GOALS OF THIS ASSIGNMENT:
To review the use of sources of secondary authority.
To emphasize how the various publications cross-reference users to other materials.

Sydney Fanning has hired the California law firm for which you are clerking to represent her. Following a stop of her automobile, Sydney was recently arrested for possession of narcotics. At the time of Sydney's arrest, officers conducted a search incident to arrest and seized Sydney's cell phone. The officers then conducted a warrantless search of the information stored in the phone.

The attorney assigned to Sydney's case has asked you to conduct some preliminary research on whether the search of a wireless communication device, such as Sydney's cell phone, is valid under the Fourth Amendment to the United States Constitution.

1. Into what broad areas of the law does this question fall?

2. Using your online catalog, find a treatise in your library on child custody. List the author, title, and date of publication.

3. Use either *HeinOnline: Law Journal Library* or *Index to Legal Periodicals & Books* in print. Find a 2008 law review article that discusses iPhones and the Fourth Amendment. The article appeared in the **UCLA Law Review**. Find the article in your library and cite it using proper Bluebook form.

4.   Another good source of secondary authority is A.L.R. Use the A.L.R. Index and find an A.L.R.6th annotation published in 2011 concerning the validity of searches of a telecommunications devices such as a wireless personal communication device. Look up the annotation and provide the citation using proper *Bluebook* form. **Tip:** Newer annotations are indexed in the pocket part.

5.   Now examine the beginning of the A.L.R. annotation. Note the different types of research references to other publications and annotations. What are the sections listed in Am. Jur. 2d where you would find a discussion under the topic *Searches and Seizures*?

6.   *American Jurisprudence 2d* may also provide background information on an area of unfamiliar law. In your library, find the topic and **first** section of Am. Jur. 2d from the sections in the answer to Question 5. Answer the following question: the Fourth Amendment prohibits only what type of searches and seizures?

ASSIGNMENT FIFTEEN
REVIEW—FINDING SECONDARY AUTHORITY
EXERCISE C

GOALS OF THIS ASSIGNMENT:
To review the use of sources of secondary authority using Westlaw.
To emphasize how the various publications cross-reference users to other materials.

Logan Bradford and Casey Davidson have hired the Indiana law firm for which you are clerking to represent them. Logan and Casey are same-sex partners who want to jointly adopt a child. The couple wants to know if domestic partners are permitted jointly to adopt a child who is not biologically related to either of them.

The attorney assigned to Logan and Casey's case has asked you to conduct some preliminary research on the issue of whether a same-sex couple may petition jointly to adopt a child who is not biologically related to either party.

Sign on to Westlaw.

Access the *Indiana Law Encyclopedia*, an Indiana secondary source, to answer Questions 1-3.

1.   Search the *Indiana Law Encyclopedia* for an entry discussing whether same-sex partners are included as persons who may adopt. What is the section under topic *Adoption*?

2.   Click on the section from Question 1. What is the cite to the Indiana law stating that the petitioner for adoption must be of sufficient ability to rear the child and furnish suitable support and education?

3.   What is the name of the 2006 Indiana Court of Appeals decision stating that same-sex couples are not prohibited under the adoption statute from filing a joint petition to adopt a child?

Access the law reviews and journals from Indiana to answer Question 4.

4.   Locate an article 2008 law review article on the Hague Convention on Intercountry Adoption and international adoptions by gay and lesbian couples. The article appeared in the **Indiana International & Comparative Law Review**. Cite the article in proper *Bluebook* form.

Next, search for a form in the Indiana Practice Series – Essential Forms, a publication of forms, on Westlaw to answer Question 5.

5.   Locate the form for a decree of adoption not involving a stepparent. Read the form. More than how many days must have expired since the court entered its order directing notice and specifying supervisory period?

Lastly, go to Indiana News to answer Question 6.

6.   Find the June 17, 2012 letter to the editor in the *Indianapolis Star* that purports to clarify the position of the American Academy of Pediatrics' policy statement on co-parent or second-parent adoption by same-sex parents. What is the name of the author of the letter to the editor?

ASSIGNMENT FIFTEEN
REVIEW—FINDING SECONDARY AUTHORITY
EXERCISE D

GOALS OF THIS ASSIGNMENT:
To review the use of sources of secondary authority using Lexis Advance.
To emphasize how the various publications cross-reference users to other materials.

Sydney Fanning has hired the Texas law firm for which you are clerking to represent her. Following a stop of her automobile, Sydney was recently arrested for possession of narcotics. At the time of Sydney's arrest, officers conducted a search incident to arrest and seized Sydney's cell phone. The officers then conducted a warrantless search of the information stored in the phone.

The attorney assigned to Sydney's case has asked you to conduct some preliminary research on whether the search of a wireless communication device, such as Sydney's cell phone, is valid under the Fourth Amendment to the United States Constitution.

Sign on to Lexis Advance.

Use content filter *American Jurisprudence 2d* to answer Questions 1-3.

1.   Search for the section dealing with permissible searches of the area within the arrestee's control during a search incident to a lawful arrest. What is the section under topic *Searches and Seizures*?

2.   Click on the section from Question 1 and read the section. The area to be searched during a search incident to arrest is limited to the arrestee's what?

3.   Look at the cases found under the Supplement section. What is the name of the 2011 United States Court of Appeals, Fifth Circuit decision that held that police officers could search the defendant's cell phone, including text messages, incident to his arrest made with a valid arrest warrant?

Use content filter to Wake Forest Law Review, a law review for a school located in North Carolina, to answer Question 4.

4.   Locate a student-written 2011 law review comment on the Fourth Amendment and warrantless cell phone searches. The comment appeared in the **Wake Forest Law Review**. Cite the article using proper *Bluebook* form.

Next, use content filter Texas forms to answer Question 5.

5.   Locate a form for a motion to suppress warrantless seizure. What is the number of the form?

Lastly, use content filter Texas Lawyer to answer Question 6.

6.   Search for articles on **cell phone data**. Who wrote the Oct. 27, 2011 article *Cell Phone Data and Expectations of Privacy*?